D1013217

Enemies in Love

Enemies in Love

A German POW, a Black Nurse, and an Unlikely Romance

Alexis Clark

THE NEW PRESS

25 YEARS

NEW YORK
LONDON

Jacket and interior photographs courtesy of Chris Albert

Requests for permission to reproduce selections from this book
should be mailed to: Permissions Department,
The New Press, 120 Wall Street, 31st floor, New York, NY 10005.

Published in the United States by The New Press, New York, 2018
Distributed by Two Rivers Distribution

ISBN 978-1-62097-186-4 (hc)
ISBN 978-1-62097-187-1 (e-book)
CIP data is available

The New Press publishes books that promote and enrich public discussion
and understanding of the issues vital to our democracy and to a more
equitable world. These books are made possible by the enthusiasm of our
readers; the support of a committed group of donors, large and small;
the collaboration of our many partners in the independent media and the
not-for-profit sector; booksellers, who often hand-sell New Press books;
librarians; and above all by our authors.

www.thenewpress.com

Book design by Lovedog Studio
Composition by dix!
This book was set in Bembo

Printed in the United States of America

2   4   6   8   10   9   7   5   3   1

To my parents,
Ben and Jennifer Clark

Contents

Author's Note

THIS IS THE NONFICTION LOVE STORY OF ELINOR Powell, an African American army nurse, and Frederick Albert, a German prisoner of war. The two met when black army nurses were put in regular contact with German POWs who were detained in the United States during World War II, an unlikely and little-discussed circumstance during one of the most documented periods in history.

I learned about Elinor Powell Albert in 2008. I became interested in black military history around that time after discovering I was a distant relative of Charles Young, the U.S. Army's first black colonel, the leader of the Buffalo Soldiers, and the highest-ranking black officer in the U.S. Army until his death in 1922.

I stumbled across a brief mention of Elinor in a book by naval historian Barbara Brooks Tomblin called *G.I. Nightingales: The Army Nurse Corps in World War II.* In a chapter about the integration of black nurses, one line changed everything I thought I knew about the war: "The Florence camp holds special memories for Albert, who met and later married one of the German prisoners interned there." Black nurses in POW camps during World War II? Nazi soldiers in the United States? I was stunned. I contacted Tomblin, who had written the book almost fifteen years prior and had no idea if Elinor was still alive. She had never met her, having found Elinor's name on a list of black nurses to whom she sent questionnaires about their war experience. I realized I would have to find out about Elinor some other way because I was definitely not ready to let go of her story.

I knew an abundance of research would be required to uncover the story of Elinor and Frederick Albert, who were both deceased. Fortunately, after describing my project and presenting a proposal to the Ford Foundation, I was awarded a series of grants. Soon after, I embarked on my research, tracking down relatives and friends in the United States and Germany, as well as sorting through historical documents. This book is the result. Every scene and conversation is drawn from the countless interviews I conducted with surviving family members and friends. Any conjecture is based on plausible scenarios supported by exhaustive archival research, including oral histories, letters, and military records. In 2013 I wrote an article about Elinor and Frederick for the *New York Times*, and the idea to expand their story into a book came shortly after.

As a black woman from Texas who was educated in predominantly white schools and at one point lived in a mostly white neighborhood, though my father grew up in Jim

Crow Louisiana, I felt a connection to Elinor, and I wanted to know everything about her. What was it like to be an African American nurse in a segregated state? How did she cope with being humiliated and mistreated by whites as an adult when, as I later discovered, her upbringing was filled with positive interactions with white people? How was it possible to love a man who was raised in a country that believed the Aryan race was superior?

Many questions remain unanswered about Elinor and Frederick's relationship and experiences in their respective armies. They were private, even reticent with their children about the war years. But their story reveals a largely unknown and tremendously compelling aspect of military history and race relations in this country. It filled me with a sense of duty to document not only her journey but the period and place in which Jim Crow and Nazism collided and the very unlikely love story it spawned that lasted more than fifty years.

Introduction

ELINOR POWELL PULLED OPEN THE HEAVY GLASS
doors and walked into the massive Woolworth's department
store on Phoenix's East Washington Street. She adjusted her
uniform, tugged at her jacket to air out some of the sweat
that drenched her back, and walked to the edge of the lunch
counter.

She could feel several white faces glaring in her direction as she stared straight ahead, waiting for the server to
approach.

"You can't sit here."

"I'd like a ginger ale, please," Elinor said, ignoring his
comment.

"I said you can't sit here. No Negroes at the counter."
The diners became silent.

"Excuse me, sir. I'm an American citizen and an officer in
the United States Army Nurse Corps. I'd like to order a ginger ale," Elinor responded, trying to contain her emotions.

"I don't care who you are. If you don't leave, I'll call the police."

Elinor felt the tears forming in the corners of her eyes, but there was no way she would break in front of this racist simpleton and a roomful of unsympathetic patrons.

She was off duty and hoping a day to herself would clear her mind. There weren't any critical cases at the hospital, and there were enough nurses on call to handle an emergency if one arose. The German prisoners of war detained at Camp Florence were faring just fine, in Elinor's eyes. In fact, they were treated better by Arizonans than were African Americans wearing U.S. military uniforms.

All she wanted was an ice-cold soda. The temperatures in Florence were well over 90 degrees, and the hour-long commute to Phoenix made her delirious with fantasies of sipping a cool drink at the downtown lunch counter. The United States Army Nurse Corps clearly hadn't considered ventilation in their uniform design. The sturdy jacket and skirt, and hat, along with the long-sleeved blouse and nylons, were a torturous ensemble in August.

Elinor saw a menu on the counter, picked it up, and threw it on the floor before storming out. If a glass had been sitting there, she would have thrown that instead. She didn't know where she was going. Her legs and brain hadn't connected yet. But she felt the tears falling off her face, which made her more enraged. There was a small restaurant not too far away. Elinor walked in and pretended not to see people stop talking in midsentence when she approached the counter. "May I help you?" asked a young waitress. It had been a long time since someone asked her that. Relieved, Elinor sat down, smiled, and asked for a ginger ale.

"Sorry, but you can't sit here. You can order around back and I'll bring it to you."

Several seconds passed before Elinor silently got up and walked out. There was no point throwing a tantrum. She had already done that today.

She guzzled a soda she bought at an old convenience store and walked into a movie theater in lieu of the shopping she had originally planned to do. Maybe a movie would take her mind off the day's heartache. But when the usher escorted Elinor to "her" section, she gave up feeling hopeful about anything once she realized he was referring to where blacks sat.

On the bus ride back she contemplated lying to the other black nurses about her miserable afternoon, but that wouldn't be right. They would go to Woolworth's thinking they could get served, only to be told to leave in front of a restaurant full of people. She wouldn't want anyone else to go through that humiliation.

At least she would make it back to the base in time for dinner. She could commiserate over her meal with the other nurses, but she didn't want anyone's pity.

When she made it to the mess hall, she was suddenly exhausted. Smiling, though preoccupied, she sat down at the nurses' table, barely noticing the conversation that flowed around her until a hush came over the table and everyone looked in her direction.

"What?" she asked. And there he was behind her. Frederick. Elinor felt her heart flutter. He was wearing his white chef's hat and apron, the same getup he'd worn the first time he approached her. Normally he remained in the kitchen while the other German POWs served the meals, but not that night.

"I made this for you." He placed a tray with a piece of piping hot apple strudel and a desert zinnia in front of her. He smiled, looking deeply into her eyes as if he knew exactly what had happened in Phoenix. "You missed lunch. I'm glad you're back," he said. Then he turned and retreated to the kitchen. Elinor was so stunned that she didn't even get a chance to thank him.

The other nurses giggled and started to pick at her strudel. She smiled. The day's degradation was suddenly a distant memory.

She went to bed thinking about Frederick, who in one instant had made her feel like a human again, a beautiful, desirable human, something she hadn't felt since she enlisted, and something she knew she wanted and needed. A German, of all people, made her feel this way. A German in Hitler's army.

Enemies in Love

1.

Elinor

Twenty-three-year-old Elinor Elizabeth Powell arrived at Fort Huachuca, a military installation in southern Arizona, with an ID number (N758592), an acceptance letter from the United States Army Nurse Corps, and a sense of relief that she was not returning to her family home in Milton, Massachusetts, to live with her demanding mother. Just a year earlier, in 1943, she had graduated from the Lincoln School for Nurses, a privately endowed institution in the Bronx, New York, founded in 1898, one of a small number of nursing schools that admitted African American women at the time.

Elinor's life in New York City couldn't have been more different from her upbringing in the white suburb of Milton. She'd become a city girl, living in Harlem, dating, partying, studying, and finishing near the top of her nursing class of thirty-nine students. The population of blacks in Harlem had been approximately 327,000 in 1930, after the first wave of migration from the South.[1] By 1940, they had been joined by thousands more, making it astronomically larger than the black population in Milton. Harlem had jazz, clubs, liquor, dancing, drugs, numbers running, and sex. The cultural influences of the Harlem Renaissance were cemented in African American culture by that time—poetry readings, "rent parties" where hosts charged entrance fees to help pay their rent, jam sessions, and NAACP meetings were regular occurrences. Elinor's new social life was unlike anything she'd ever experienced before.

She now stood on the desolate grounds of Fort Huachuca, breathing in the thick hot air and taking in the 360-degree view of the mountains and desert with amazement and mild trepidation. She was in the middle of no-man's-land as a brand-new addition to the United States Army. Joining the military was a way of asserting authority over her life at the time, as well as carrying on her beloved father's legacy of serving the country during wartime. Arizona—a western state that adhered to Jim Crow doctrine, which oppressed African Americans nationwide but most pervasively in the Deep South—was worlds away from anything Elinor had ever known growing up. Her skin color hadn't been much of a problem in her progressive, solidly middle-class hometown, but as she made her way to the formation line for nurses and saw the separate hospitals for blacks and whites, she suddenly realized that the transition before her would be more extreme than she'd anticipated.

~

THE ATTRACTIVE Dutch colonial with the meticulously manicured yard at 33 Emerson Road was similar to most of the houses on the street—a wholesome-looking single-family, two-story dwelling with a narrow driveway and lush shrubbery that lined the steps to the front door. Emerson Road was in Milton, a white upper-middle-class suburb of Boston, with a rich history dating back to the Puritans' arrival in the late seventeenth century. According to the 1940 census, William L. Powell, age fifty-four, lived in the house with his wife, Gladys, forty-four, and their three daughters: Gladys, twenty, Elinor, nineteen, and Ruth, seventeen. William, who went by his middle name, Lawrence, listed his occupation as "government clerk" and his wife as not employed—the same status that had been selected for all the other wives in the neighborhood. Lawrence recorded his home's value at $5,000 and his annual income at $2,100, a few hundred more than the salaries of some of his neighbors who worked as salesmen, cooks, or clerks in the shipyard.[2]

Nothing about Lawrence Powell's personal data seemed unusual except for one particular detail. Unlike the other residents of Emerson Road, a "W" did not follow the entry that identified the family's race. Instead, the abbreviation "Neg" appeared. The Powells were the only blacks on Emerson Road and one of the few African American families in Milton at the time.

Lawrence Powell was a son of William I. Powell, a barber, and Ellen "Ella" Wade, a former slave from Winchester, Virginia, who escaped around the age of fourteen through the Underground Railroad to Maine, where she worked as a domestic for a white family, according to great-great-grandchildren who recorded the family history.[3] When the Caucasian family from Maine moved to East Milton, Ella went with them. The date and circumstances of how she met her future husband, William Powell, aren't known, but the two married in Boston in 1874. William was born in Baltimore, Maryland, and made his way to Milton, where in addition to cutting hair he worked as a porter and master craftsman.[4] He and Ella lived at 114 Granite Place in a massive white Colonial Revival structure built on a granite foundation. It was a grand house with stately navy blue shutters—a residence not typically associated with a former slave and barber toward the end of Reconstruction. Records from the Massachusetts Historical Commission listed the home in 1876 as the Littlefield/Powell house. Samuel Littlefield was a successful carriage maker and lived in an estate on nearby Milton Hill, in addition to owning a stretch of land on Granite Place that included the grand house where William and Ella lived. The exact relationship between the Powells and the Littlefield family wasn't officially recorded in real estate records, but given the times, the Powells were likely loyal employees who inherited the house from Littlefield.

After his passing in 1874, Ella and William eventually

became the sole owners of the sprawling residence, making them one of the first black families to ever own a house in Milton, let alone on prominent Granite Place, where they were the only black residents and where they remained until their deaths decades later.

The Powells, who had two sons, Albert, born in 1875, and Lawrence, born in 1886, had a favorable reputation within the community. William was known for his talent in architecture and was credited with building a colonial-style home at 102 Granite Place, just a stone's throw from the main house. Ella and William lived a life that very few African Americans could ever dream of having. William's considerable confidence and his work ethic were traits that the next generations of Powells would emulate.[5]

He and Ella, as African Americans originally from the South, had difficult backgrounds, but they assimilated and thrived in Milton. In his obituary from the *Milton Record* on May 24, 1924, William I. Powell was described as a person "held in high regard by his neighbors and friends who came to know his amiable disposition." He had been an employee for forty years at Tubular Rivet and Stud Company in nearby Wollaston, where he was also active in Wollaston's Methodist Church, and he was a member of Milton's fire department.[6]

There was only a minuscule population of blacks in Boston in the late nineteenth century, but Ella and William managed to build a prosperous life for themselves. To assimilate into a white upper-middle-class community where they had once most likely served as domestics meant they had to have been resilient, focused, and faithful individuals. It also meant that Milton was a town that didn't discriminate toward or oppress blacks—at least not in any institutional way, which would have forbidden the Powells from owning a home or William from working for the city's fire department. Milton symbolized progress and autonomy—values ingrained in the people who had settled there more than two hundred years before Ella and William Powell would arrive.

Milton was founded in 1640 by the Puritans; there are multiple theories about the origin of the town name, but the most plausible one is that it was named in honor of Milton Abbey in Dorset, England.[7] The town was ideally located bordering bustling Boston between the Neponset River and the Blue Hills Reservation—a stretch of seven thousand hillside acres ripe for logging—and so it attracted wealthy entrepreneurs and investors. Originally an agrarian community with farms, Milton transformed into an industrial mecca with railway access to Boston and numerous mills, including a gristmill, gunpowder mill, and paper mill. It also had a chocolate mill, Walter Baker & Company, which has been called one of the first manufacturers of chocolate in the United States.[8]

Milton's place in history was cemented toward the end of the eighteenth century, leading right up to the Revolutionary War. The people of Massachusetts wanted independence and the ability to produce and move commerce without stringent taxes. They also wanted to choose their own governing council. England found these demands rebellious and instituted draconian laws in response. And the colony of Massachusetts responded in kind. In 1774 Milton became home to the Suffolk Resolves, a number of resolutions signed by leaders of Suffolk County that directly pushed back against the British government's continued attempt to disenfranchise the people of Massachusetts. The aggressive wording signaled the growing animosity between the colonies and England and was considered a foundation for what would become the Declaration of Independence.[9] From its inception, the DNA of Milton was progressive and independent, and the spirit of that autonomy carried on into the next century, when Ella and William, freed from their own bondage and oppression, respectively, moved to Milton to build a new life.

The Powells couldn't have chosen a better town to raise a black family, although neighboring Boston wasn't as welcoming. Boston, as a whole, lacked diversity. According to the 1880 census, 356,826 whites lived there. "Colored" people, as listed in the census, included blacks, Chinese, and Native Americans, and totaled just 6,013 residents.[10]

Despite Boston being one of the largest American cities, the black population there continued to lag. In 1890, there were 8,125 blacks; by 1920, there were 16,350. Although the black population had doubled in those 30 years, it comprised only 1.8 to 2.3 percent of Boston's entire population.[11]

The few blacks who did live there rarely flourished

individually or collectively. Most were victims of persistent job discrimination, residential segregation, and social prejudice. Often, blacks who migrated north for a better life had the double blow of having to compete in the job market with European immigrants as well as northern-born blacks.[12] Menial jobs—bootblack, janitor, coachman, cook— were the default career options for most African Americans in Boston from the turn of the century until World War II, making the Powells' trajectory all the more impressive.

But Boston was a complex city, and a suburb such as Milton could operate under a different value system in which blacks such as William and Ella Powell, and later their son, Lawrence, could live comfortably without any threats. Boston proper could not boast the same level of racial tolerance.

In the early 1800s there were violent race riots against the Irish in Boston. But when blacks from the South began to arrive, they found themselves on the receiving end of this intense prejudice, which was not unlike the racism they experienced in the South. In the North whites also resorted to tactics that reinforced their social, economic, and political superiority over the black population. In public places, whether for entertainment or dining, blacks were segregated to remote and inadequate corners or excluded altogether. If traveling by train, blacks were forced to sit in the "Negro" car. If traveling by boat, blacks were relegated to the deck irrespective of weather. Charles Lenox Remond, the nineteenth-century Massachusetts-born African American orator and abolitionist, said that he nearly froze to death on

such a journey. Frederick Douglass once spoke about being turned away from an exhibit on the Boston Common,
which had always been a public space. In the early twentieth century African Americans were also regularly vulnerable to acts of violence by white individuals. Packs of
white youths hunted down blacks on the Boston Common
to physically brutalize and hurl insults at them.[13]

Where Boston differed from the Deep South was the
emerging and passionate anti-racist community that was
ready to combat bigotry. An alliance between socially
conscious blacks and white liberals formed in pockets of
Boston communities, and together they advocated for black
equality and civil rights at the beginning of the twentieth
century. By 1918, the Boston branch of the NAACP was
the largest in the country, with a membership of 2,553 people. Although mostly black, the group also included whites,
typically descendants of abolitionists, who grew up promot-
ing an anti-slavery agenda.[14] This activism began to spread
throughout major northeastern cities, and by the time Lawrence Powell was an adult, he had taken full advantage of
every opportunity that came his way as an African American male.

Lawrence demonstrated leadership qualities and ambi-
tion while growing up. He was tall, lean, and athletic, with
chocolate brown skin and a narrow, handsome face with
high cheekbones. At Milton High School and Cunningham
Gym, Lawrence was captain of the basketball team, and he
excelled in baseball, football, and track. When he graduated,

he apprenticed and learned how to operate and repair elevator machinery, then took a job as an elevator operator at the Boston Custom House, a good, solid occupation that paid decently.[15]

After the United States entered the Great War in 1917, Lawrence dutifully enlisted in the United States Army to honor his country. He wouldn't be the first Powell to serve. A relative, John Powell, had been in the 39th United States Colored Troops (USCT) Regiment Infantry in Baltimore for the Union Army in 1864–1865, during the Civil War.[16] Once Lawrence cleared his physical, he left Milton and moved to Camp Zachary Taylor in Louisville, Kentucky, as different from Massachusetts as any state could get.

Camp Zachary Taylor, named after the twelfth president, was once the country's largest training facility for soldiers during World War I. Kentucky was a former slave state, and every aspect of its society was completely segregated; the U.S. military was no exception. And the role of black men in the army was minimized and diminished, similar to their standing in society. Ray Elliott, an African American veteran whose father fought in the Great War, learned about the racist treatment his father received in the army. "Growing up, my dad never talked about his experience," said Elliott. His father was in the 92nd Division, the all-black regiment in the United States military sent to France under the direction of the French military because no American commander wanted to be in charge of black troops. "They felt that they weren't good warriors and not good fighters, so . . . the French government took them under their command, and it was very exciting the fact that his regiment performed so meritoriously that the French government awarded them, the highest honor, the Croix de Guerre." [17]

But most black soldiers, including Lawrence, didn't see combat or serve overseas during the Great War. They usually maintained equipment or provided some labor reinforcement, roles typically without fanfare, prestige, or authority, let alone opportunities to rise through the ranks. For Milton-born Lawrence, who had enjoyed a comfortable and liberal upbringing, Kentucky would have been his first real encounter with a southern state and its mores. But if there were incidents of racism by white commanding officers or local Louisville residents stationed near the base, it had little impact on Lawrence, because he excelled in the army. In 1918, he was commissioned as a second lieutenant, garnering him a mention in the *Milton Record* with the headline " 'Larry' Powell Wins Commission." [18]

Despite the fanfare at home and his promotion, Lawrence was still black and Kentucky was still the South, and by default he would have to adhere to enforced segregation and second-class citizenship. Jim Crow was the law, and the lynching of black men was commonplace after Reconstruction, peaking during the 1890s, with spikes until the 1920s. A report by the Equal Justice Initiative concludes that between 1877 and 1950, 4,075 black people were killed by "racial terror lynchings" in a dozen states, including Kentucky.[19] Even as a lieutenant, Lawrence still couldn't socialize in the officers' club—a space exclusively for white officers—and he still had to drink from "colored" water fountains throughout the state. Eating at restaurants was also off-limits. Most socializing for African Americans was done at church or local dances held for African American troops where devout and educated African Americans congregated.

It was at one of these local dances that Second Lieutenant Lawrence Powell met his future wife. Gladys Farrow was an outspoken, big-boned, brown-skinned woman born in 1896 into a large, close-knit, educated family of African Americans from Murray, Kentucky. She was a schoolteacher and a college graduate.

Although Lawrence didn't have a degree, he was an officer in the army, which made him a highly attractive prospect for any woman. Plus he looked regal in his official army uniform. The jodhpurs, riding boots, and single-breasted tunic jacket with the army detail on his shoulder commanded respect. The two quickly fell in love.

Gladys was almost twenty-three years old at the time—in that era, an eyebrow-raising age for a single woman without a steady boyfriend—which probably made accepting Lawrence's marriage proposal a bit easier despite the fact that he had less education than she did. But if marrying late wasn't shocking enough, Gladys did the unthinkable and left her beloved family in Kentucky to settle in Milton with Lawrence's people in 1918. It was a painful decision, but Gladys was a hopeless romantic, and so she agreed to move to where the Powells had established themselves comfortably. She was also likely influenced by the absence of Jim Crow in Milton and the fact that they could live with Lawrence's parents in their spacious house and shop at the same stores and send their kids to the same schools as their white neighbors. She and Lawrence settled in the Powell family house on 114 Granite Place and started their own family almost immediately, having three daughters; Gladys, in 1919, Elinor, in 1921, and Ruth, in 1922.

The move to Massachusetts was a shock for Gladys. "She was from a huge southern family," said her great-granddaughter Alethea Felton. "The Powells were affluent people, but there weren't a lot of southern blacks around her and the culture was very different. She was extremely homesick."

From the late 1800s to early 1920s, "marriage bars" were commonplace in the United States. This practice restricted married women from working in particular professions, or sometimes from working at all. Massachusetts, despite its growing number of women activists and suffragettes, didn't support married women as schoolteachers, and local school boards usually shunned any who applied for employment.[20] This meant all of the education and training that Gladys had so proudly earned was useless in Milton. In the early twentieth century, teaching positions were given to young, single women without children. A married woman's job was to tend to her husband and kids, while the man of the house dutifully provided for his family. And Lawrence did just that. He found a steady government job as a clerk. By 1935, he had made enough money to move his family from Granite Place into their own house, ten minutes away, on Emerson Road. As a government employee, he was spared unemployment during the Great Depression and was even able to help those less fortunate in his community.

"They didn't lose anything, as a matter of fact," said Hope Taylor, a Powell grandchild. "They helped take care of a lot of neighbors in terms of sharing food and that kind of thing." [21]

Lawrence and Gladys had all of the attributes of the perfect American family: three beautiful and healthy children, their own home, and even a dog. Gladys, who would resent not being able to continue her work as a schoolteacher, delved into motherhood, chronicling her children's progress from the start. In Elinor's baby book, she wrote, "Elinor has begun to move about. She is sitting up on her own. She seems to laugh at Gladys. And she doesn't like strawberry." [22]

Just like William and Ella, the next generation, Lawrence and Gladys, were living a life that reflected a high level of stability, an attribute not typically associated with black households in the early twentieth century and certainly not during the throes of the Great Depression. There were two factions of blacks in Boston: the small group of lawyers, doctors, businessmen, intellectual elites, and other professionals; and the majority who lived in overcrowded, tenement squalor. [23]

The Powells, shielded from urban blight, had been lucky to

set up roots in Milton. Family photos show Gladys sitting in her white-picket-fenced backyard with flowers in full bloom, surrounded by her three daughters all wearing summer dresses with floral motifs, patent-leather shoes, and ribbons and decorative clips adorning their hair. Home ownership among the black population was still very rare, but if there was any resentment from white neighbors about the Powells' success, it wasn't expressed, at least not in a significant way. Other photos show Elinor, in a polka-dot dress, sitting in the parlor with two of her white friends reading *Life* magazine.

Perhaps because she wasn't able to devote her time to paid work, Gladys spent a great deal of effort engaging her daughters in extracurricular activities and involving herself in community work. She and Lawrence wanted their children exposed to the same academic, social, and civic activities they had enjoyed growing up, if not more. Gladys became very involved in the community for her daughters' benefit as well as her own. And her true love became the Girl Scouts of America. In fact, Gladys was single-handedly responsibly for integrating the Girl Scout troop in Milton when she insisted that her daughters be allowed on an overnight camping trip, which had never before included black Girl Scouts. When she passed away many years later, a tribute to her dedication as a Girl Scout leader appeared in the *Milton Record* on June 4, 1948:

In the death of Gladys Powell, Milton Girl Scouting has lost one of its most able leaders, one who did much to build Girl Scouting in Milton to its present strong position. Mrs. Powell became leader of Troop 4, the first troop in the East Milton section.... She was the only colored woman as a leader of predominantly white troops in the United States—a symbol of Girl Scouting at its best, and a tribute to her exceptional personality and ability.

Gladys had a strong demeanor and had no tolerance for any hint of inequality. "She was an activist, like a feminist of her day and was against any type of racism," said Alethea. "In today's terms, she'd be considered a little bit crazy. She was very brazen for her time period and she didn't care, particularly around white people. She was extremely outspoken about injustice toward her children. She had to be that way coming from the Deep South."

Once her daughter Ruth came home and mentioned that she had been given a role in a play at the local theater company. "Which one?" Gladys asked. In addition to being active in Girl Scouts, Gladys was director of Community Dramatics and Pageants for the city of Milton and did all of the costumes for them. Ruth replied, "I'm going to be a servant." Gladys snapped. She took her rifle and marched down to the theater. The story is told that she raised her gun at the director and producer and said, "My child will not be a maid! You will make her the lead in your play." They gave Ruth the role, and a white child was the maid instead.

Gladys wasn't just outspoken; she could be a bully. It was no secret that she missed her family terribly back home in the South. Milton never provided the large family closeness that she had grown accustomed to having in Kentucky. Her inability to work outside the home because she was a married woman with children was a major source of tension within her own marriage. Consequently Gladys became resentful and confrontational toward Lawrence, frequently putting him down even though he provided well for his family. Her dominant personality and persistent degrading of Lawrence, who was soft-spoken, had a negative impact on her girls.

"She would talk to him in a way that made the girls angry and resent her," said Hope. Whether it was at the dinner table or sitting together in the parlor, Gladys would lay into Lawrence right in front of her daughters while he sat quiet and emasculated. And Gladys's dominant, bullying behavior created bad feelings among the girls themselves, feelings that were not openly expressed but nevertheless very present in their childhood.

~

ELINOR WAS confident like her mother and evoked an air of self-assurance when she walked in a room. As a teenager she would grow to be six feet tall, and she was usually the tallest girl wherever she went, standing with impeccable posture and wearing well-tailored dresses. In the 1938 Milton High School yearbook, Elinor was recognized for her participation in extracurricular activities. She was the only African American student in her grade, but that had no impact on her psychologically. She, like her mother, Gladys, would join whatever group interested her, without ever letting race be a determining factor. Elinor was in the French Club, Biology Club, and Glee Club, and co-wrote the "Class Prophecy" for the graduating seniors. The essay, a cleverly composed and humorous prediction about the career path of each of her classmates, including how they would all reunite twenty years later, flowed from the hand of a free and self-assured spirit, not from someone held back by racial discrimination or isolation.

Living in Milton spared Elinor the indignities being reported in the black newspapers of the day—lynchings, poor housing, segregation, substandard schools. In her yearbook, her classmates wrote, "She injects a few raisins of conversation in the tasteless dough of existence. Elinor's flow of ready wit has given her friends many a riotous moment in a dull study hour." [24] She was quick-witted and sociable and was able to develop a healthy sense of confidence and self-worth. And like her mother, Elinor was also ambitious and wanted a career. She dreamed of becoming a veterinarian and, in fact, predicted she would become one in the class prophecy she wrote for herself. [25]

Yet Gladys wasn't keen on Elinor's lofty career aspirations, a fact that laid the foundation for mounting friction between mother and daughter. As a southern-born woman who was all too familiar with Jim Crow, Gladys discouraged Elinor from moving away from her support system to pursue a dream that she viewed as too ambitious for a black woman. In her journal Elinor's older sister, Gladys, wrote that she recalled their mother telling Elinor "that unless she wanted to work in the stockyards with cattle in the Midwest, she could forget about becoming a veterinarian." She wanted her daughters to aim high but not so far that they could face a bitter reality as black women. Moreover, she was anxious about her daughters moving away from her.

After graduating with honors from Milton High, Elinor chose to attend nursing school, a decision influenced by her mother's overbearing nature. That she decided to move out of state was a product of the sad reality that not many nursing schools in the United States were even open to black students. And yet, by choosing the Lincoln School for Nurses in the Bronx, Elinor made a good decision. Lincoln was a highly respected medical institution with a beautifully equipped facility and an excellent staff.[26]

She excelled in her nursing studies and relished the independent life in New York City. Not all of her adventures were positive, but even the more questionable ones further developed her confidence in her ability to take care of herself. Once she found herself on a date with a smooth-talking man dressed in a zoot suit. It was her first time out with a New York City guy, and the student nurse from the Boston suburbs was excited to be wooed by a grown man. He drove his shiny car deep into the Bronx, parts of which were still quite rural at the time, stopped the car, and whipped out his penis. Elinor, in a fit of tears, managed to talk her way out of the shocking encounter, but it left a deep impression.[27]

She couldn't have been further away from the world of Girl Scouts and the careful watch of her mother in Milton. She was on her own in New York City.

When Elinor graduated in 1943 she was one of the top ten students in her class. She'd also developed into a striking woman with a statuesque, curvaceous shape and beautiful smile. She favored her father in looks: both had high cheekbones, a dark chocolate complexion, and alluring eyes. She confidently posed for photos wearing her white nurse's uniform: a white dress and apron with white stockings and white leather nurse shoes. She must have been pondering her future. With a nursing degree in hand, she did have choices, but she was a single African American woman and it was 1943, so there were many factors that needed to be considered.

Everything changed that year: Lawrence Powell died at the age of fifty-six from complications of hypertension. Medications for high cholesterol and high blood pressure weren't as advanced or readily available as they are nowadays, and succumbing to such illnesses wasn't uncommon, particularly for black people who had limited health care options. To lose this tender, kind, and soft-spoken parent was an unimaginable blow to the family. Gladys was now a widow at the age of forty-seven. Her eldest daughter was working for the Red Cross in Arizona. Elinor, just twenty-two, was in New York. And her youngest daughter was a student at Howard University in Washington, D.C.

Gladys was now alone, something she had dreaded ever since leaving her large family in Kentucky.

With a nursing degree in hand, Elinor had decisions to make about her future. She could work at a hospital in Boston and live at home with her mother. A single woman didn't live by herself if she had family close by, let alone if her mother was a widow. But moving back home after spending three years living independently in New York City wasn't an attractive proposition. For one, the thought of living in the family home without her father and under her mother's very close watch seemed oppressive.

She also didn't relish the idea of working at an under-funded and overcrowded city hospital. Elinor knew that despite her comfortable upbringing and good education, there was a strong chance that if she stayed in Boston, she'd be relegated to a low-paying nursing job with limited advancement and lower wages.

She would very likely run into the same problems in New York. In the early 1940s, Elinor could find work in a New York City hospital that accepted black medical staff, but she would be paid significantly less than whites who held the same positions. She would also most likely be forced to live in racially segregated neighborhoods in Manhattan or the other boroughs, or a bit farther north in the black areas of Westchester County.

Joining the military had first crossed her mind when she heard about black nurses being accepted into the U.S. Army

Nurse Corps in 1941, before the attack on Pearl Harbor. But when the United States entered World War II the idea of enlisting became more personal. She'd always been very proud of her father's service, and following in his footsteps may have become more important to her after his death. There were only a handful of black women in the Nurse Corps, just 160 by 1943, unlike the Women's Army Auxiliary Corps, which accepted thousands of blacks, although in segregated units. But Elinor wasn't easily discouraged by the low numbers, and having been raised almost exclusively among white people, she wasn't uncomfortable with the prospect of being a minority in any given situation.

Not completely ready to make a decision, she remained in Harlem for one more year, working as a nurse. But in 1944, the time came to make a move. Elinor Elizabeth Powell enlisted in the U.S. Army Nurse Corps to carry on her father's legacy of service. Her acceptance letter, dated July 21, "by command of Major General Terry," instructed her to report to Fort Huachuca to complete her basic training.

Nothing, however, prepared her for what awaited her in the Arizona desert.

2.

Frederick

HE LIKED LEAVING THE BARRACKS WHEN IT WAS still pitch black outside. The desert heat was bearable and he could focus on his own thoughts instead of acting as the default translator for his comrades who couldn't understand their American captors. Frederick Albert was in his own world as he made his way silently along the path to the mess hall every morning at four to prepare breakfast. If Florence, Arizona, had one redeeming quality, it was the peace that came from being in the middle of nowhere. Which is exactly where Frederick was: in an American camp for German prisoners of war in 1944, thousands of miles from home.

Although he had fond memories of watching his mother prepare *brötchen*, or bread rolls, it wasn't so much the pleasure he derived from working in the kitchen that made his assigned job satisfying. Frederick relished the solitude and independence. He also loved the technical aspects of baking. Everything had to be precise and perfect, forcing him to concentrate. Time in the kitchen also meant he got to listen to U.S. Armed Forces Radio and something he had been denied by Hitler since the war started—jazz. He always hoped Louis Armstrong's rendition of "Ain't Misbe-havin' " would play. It put him in a good mood, like he had something to look forward to when he actually didn't. He was happy to be alive after being captured, but that's where the joy ended. As the black sky turned navy blue, Frederick would put on his white apron and cook's hat, turn up the volume on the radio, and take the bowl of yeast out of the refrigerator to start the bread.

Friedrich Karl Josef Albert couldn't have been born at a more fragile time in modern German history. He arrived on August 20, 1925, with wispy blond hair and gray eyes—a perfect baby, in his mother's opinion. He was the second child born to his parents, Karl and Margarete, who lived with their five-year-old daughter, Charlotte, in Oppeln, an eastern German city that had shuffled between German, Slavic, and Polish rule since the eighth century. Bordering the Oder River, Oppeln had strategic importance as a port and rail junction, but it was also known as a manufacturing center for cement, metals, and machinery—industries that would eventually make Karl Albert a very wealthy man.[1]

Frederick, as he would later be called, and his family lived comfortably in a large apartment that took up the entire floor of a building. By outward appearances, they were seemingly sheltered from the devastating effects of the Great War, which crippled most of Germany. Margarete, an elegant and aristocratic woman, decorated the home with dark wood furniture, paintings of European landscapes, and a prominent deep strawberry-colored velvet sofa. "My mother was a woman of taste, and she furnished the apartment according to the style which was then in fashion, of course," said Charlotte Tutsek, Frederick's sister. There was even a pond that Karl created to embellish the apartment building's exterior.

Margarete knew she was a stunning woman, and she took great pains to maintain her beauty. She was formal and followed strict rules of dress: never wearing pants except for a pair of ski trousers and never leaving the house without stockings and gloves. Karl provided well for his family, but he was emotionally detached and took no interest in his wife or two children. He didn't even bother to hide his affairs. Margarete responded by focusing on herself and her appearance. While Karl was away working or spending the weekend with his mistress, Margarete carried on like a woman who had many interests and was unaffected by a betrayal happening right under her nose. She liked to read a lot, mostly novels and detective stories, and enjoyed baking, cooking, and gardening. And she loved to travel, mostly in Germany, visiting friends and relatives. But spending quality time with her children rarely fit in with her plans.

Karl Albert, born around 1896 in the East German town of Magdeburg, had two interests: business and women. He was tall, handsome, charming, and a man's man. He had been a lieutenant in World War I and was a strong, no-nonsense doer. As a young engineer he worked in a factory on the outskirts of Oppeln where he developed materials used to create cement. Margarete was born in the late 1890s to an upper-class family in Siegen, in western Germany. Her father was a forest ranger and successful hunter and her mother's family owned a furniture company. Karl and Margarete thrived in Oppeln and were lucky to maintain and grow their wealth during a time when most Germans were barely getting by.

The aftermath of World War I laid the groundwork for Germany's collision course with mass poverty and political extremism. When Germany was defeated by the Allied forces in 1918 and saw its monarchy dissolved and replaced by the Weimar Republic, a parliamentary government, life as everyone had known it was over. The strict terms of the Treaty of Versailles, the peace agreement that Britain, France, and the other Allied powers set forth as Germany's punishment for waging war, was signed in 1919 and obliterated the German economy. Specifically, the treaty's Article 231, commonly referred to as the "war guilt clause," stipulated, "The Allied and Associated Governments affirm and Germany accepts responsibility of Germany and her allies for causing all the loss and damage to which the Allied and Associated Governments and their nationals have been subjected as a consequence of the war imposed upon them by the aggression of Germany and her allies." Germany was obliged to pay approximately $31.5 billion in reparations for the economic damages it caused during the war and make significant territorial concessions.[2] Consequently, Germany lost all of its colonies, 13 percent of its territory in Europe, and almost all of its military equipment, and its army was restricted to 100,000 men.[3] The draconian provisions of the peace agreement incensed many Germans, including Adolf Hitler, who resented that Germany surrendered in the first place.

Not only did the Treaty of Versailles break Germany's economy, it also destroyed the morale of the German people, who could no longer make ends meet. Inflation sky-rocketed until the United States provided another way for Germany to pay back its war debts. In 1924, at the request of the Allied Reparations Committee, the prominent Chicago banker Charles Dawes investigated the terms of Germany's agreement and recommended an increase in foreign loans to Germany and a reorganization of the German state bank. Adolf Hitler, a veteran of the Great War and an emerging voice in the Nazi Party, opposed the Dawes Plan because he claimed it gave foreigners control over Germany's economy and didn't reduce the amount of outstanding reparations. However, the plan managed to get inflation under control and strengthen the German economy. By 1928, the unemployment rate in Germany had dropped significantly.[4]

Growing up in the Albert family came with a great deal of isolation despite the abundance of material comforts most Germans could only dream of having at the time, including a spacious apartment, household staff, and vacations on the North Sea. But Karl and Margarete were distant and removed in their own ways, and both parents were also strict disciplinarians, particularly Margarete, who spanked her children with a cane, according to Charlotte. Nurturing didn't come easily for Margarete, and Charlotte didn't snuggle with her mom, play dress-up in her beautiful clothes, come home crying to her if a schoolmate was cruel, or share much about her crushes, goals, or dreams. If anyone ever received affection, it was Frederick, whom his family affectionately called "Frika."

The factory where Karl worked was not conveniently located for a young family with kids. Although the Alberts' apartment was close by and Karl had a short commute, the school that Frederick and Charlotte attended was quite a distance away. "There were no other kids around. And my mother never invited other children for birthday cake or something back then. We were alone," said Charlotte. "And we always walked to school alone, back and forth, forty-five minutes each way, by foot, no bicycle." For entertainment, Charlotte and Frederick would hang out around the factory and talk to the adults who worked there. Once they shut down the electricity by playing with the circuits and exposed cables. "They were repairing something and no one told us. Frederick could have been killed!" Their world consisted of school, playing in the factory, and painting, a hobby both siblings loved well into adulthood. In their structured and isolated world, they had a privileged though lonely childhood, while the rest of Germany struggled around them.

When Wall Street crashed in October 1929, so did Germany's economy. The country relied heavily on U.S. investments, and when the United States began to recall its loans, Germany hit rock bottom immediately. Before the stock market crashed, 1.25 million Germans were unemployed. By 1930, nearly 4 million were out of work, about 15.3 percent of the population. Many people had to rely exclusively on part-time work, and those working full-time had to accept lower wages. By 1932, more than 30 percent of the German workforce couldn't find jobs.[5]

Hitler, who had not been taken seriously by any German with influence before the crash, suddenly had a growing audience. As the leader of the National Socialist German Workers' Party, he vowed to end unemployment in Germany. Having predicted economic disaster when the Dawes Plan was put into effect, he was listened to when he spoke to a broken nation desperate for a leader who could salvage the economy. What started as a right-wing discussion that scapegoated Jews and chastised the German government for its defeat in the Great War and agreement to the Treaty of Versailles catapulted into the country rallying around Hitler's leadership.

The Alberts continued to go about their daily lives as if nothing about Germany's new leader was out of the ordinary. The rhetoric, the new pledges to Germany and the Führer—Margarete and Karl didn't say a word against any of it. But the climate had changed, and the treatment of the Jews in the small town of Oppeln had changed too. Oppeln had a small Jewish population, 607 people in 1930. By 1936 that number had dwindled to 453 as anti-Jewish hostilities increased along with Hitler's rhetoric.[6]

The Alberts' time in Oppeln lasted until Frederick was eight years old. Karl then temporarily uprooted the family to the southern town of Ulm for a short-term work opportunity. But the biggest and most significant move came around 1935, when the Alberts relocated to Vienna, Austria.

Vienna was just what a capital city should be: glamorous and culturally influential, with renowned artists, musicians, and a celebrated art academy, and with beautiful streets and squares that were architecturally and aesthetically superior to those in any other Austrian town.

The family moved into a huge apartment in an immaculate and impressive baroque-style building near the center of the city. Although they had always had housekeepers, in Vienna Karl and Margarete added a luxury car and a driver as well. Their chauffeur-driven dark blue BMW confirmed their social standing. The building had an elevator, and they hired more staff to maintain the apartment.

Just as in Oppeln, however, outside appearance didn't reflect the unhappiness inside. Both Frederick and Charlotte were deprived of emotional support from their parents, particularly from Karl, who was never around. He always preferred to wine and dine a mistress than to sit at home with his family asking about his children's school or his wife's goings-on. The simple truth was that Karl's family ranked low on his list of priorities, and it affected Frederick very deeply. Engineering and business weren't of any interest to him, but a relationship with his father certainly was. "My father was an officer in the reserves, and a bit derisive," said Charlotte. He was a believer in Germany's superiority and had little time for alternative points of view. His family obeyed whatever rules and regulations the Third Reich commanded, period. There were no exceptions because the Führer knew best.

In 1935, Hitler instituted the Nuremberg Laws, a racist set of statutes that resulted in the loss of citizenship for Jews and ban of marriages between Jews and non-Jewish Germans. But Karl and Margarete didn't give any indication to Frederick and Charlotte that their lives were in danger or that anything about the direction of the country was warped. And there was absolutely no mention of Jews. "The Jewish question was never touched," said Charlotte. It wasn't as though Frederick and Charlotte were forbidden to have Jewish friends, or that Karl and Margarete spoke ill of Jews in front of their children. But they also didn't defend them, voice any outrage over the deportations they knew were taking place, or, in fact, speak much of them at all.

Except once. On one particular morning, Karl joined his family for a meal, a rare occasion. He almost never ate with them, particularly on the weekends, because he was always with his girlfriends. Margarete usually slept late, leaving Charlotte and Frederick to eat alone. Having all four together for a morning meal made the occasion all the more memorable. Karl took his chair at the head of the table, with

Frederick and Charlotte looking at each other and wondering why he was there. "I saw the Gluckmann girl at the train station," he said, leaning in to whisper. He had seen Jews standing on the platform waiting to be deported. "I saw one of the daughters," he said, referring to a schoolmate of Charlotte's who was a few years older. Charlotte and Frederick knew why their father was whispering: a nosy housekeeper could have overheard the conversation and reported Karl to the police for talking about the Third Reich. No one in the family was to discuss the incident again.[7] They just proceeded with breakfast: Margaret sipped her coffee and the children ate their food, a typical German breakfast of bread, rolls, butter, sausage, ham, jam, and boiled eggs. They carried on, like everyone else, as Jewish families were being rounded up and taken away.

Karl and Margarete focused their attention not on the Third Reich's increasing authoritarianism, not on their children, but on wealth and good living. Although they had a loveless marriage, Margarete and Karl were an admired couple who managed to maintain a public image of a happy and unproblematic marriage.

Margarete was quite popular among the other wives in Vienna's social circles, and she fit in easily because she was beautiful, cultured, and wealthy. She had many friends, some of whom she had kept in touch with since her school days in Westphalia, and she was great at what later would come to be called networking. Whenever she went someplace or met a new person, she knew what to talk about and how to be engaging. And she and Karl would go to great lengths to entertain powerful guests.[8] Karl could attract important people both because of his success in business and because of his background in the military, and he did show loyalty to the party out of respect and as a means of survival. Though Karl and Margarete didn't belong to the Nazi Party, they both respected Hitler as a leader and supported his plans for a great German empire. They were not interested in the obligations of party membership, however, and displayed just enough patriotism and rhetoric to escape suspicion and criticism.[9]

Frederick and Charlotte loved Vienna just as much as their parents did, not least because it meant they were no longer isolated. It was an ideal environment in which they could pursue their mutual love of painting, and each found the architecture and museums inspiring. But once again they were left to themselves at a time in their lives when both longed for structure and reassurance. Radical changes were taking place all around them and the country was on the verge of war, but nothing about Margarete or Karl's routine changed.

Both Charlotte and Frederick retreated further and further into their own worlds. Any somberness or awkwardness they felt or exhibited didn't seem to concern their parents at all. Karl's reputation as an important businessman was solidified. He was on the management board of Veitscher Magnesitwerke, a major refractory company in eastern Europe that produced fire-resistant materials for the cement and steel industries—the very materials that would be invaluable in World War II. His business acumen saved him. With Karl's wealth, social standing, and business interests that benefited the war efforts, his lack of Nazi party affiliation was never questioned. He was savvy, persuasive, and likeable, and successfully maintained his apolitical stance by staying laser-focused on his career. There was something irresistible about Karl, who knew how to adapt to any environment seamlessly, and how to engage in nationalistic rhetoric to keep the heat off, if necessary. He convinced everyone around him that he was indispensable to his profession, which made him indispensable to the German army. And as a reservist and veteran, he was in close enough proximity to the war to never be accused of being unpatriotic.

Frederick and Charlotte functioned like most teenagers in the late 1930s: they went to school, had friendships, and experienced crushes. Even though they didn't speak up about what was happening around them, both of them knew that Jews were being rounded up and sent to concentration camps. The evacuations and outward displays of anti-Semitism couldn't be ignored, but it would have been unimaginable for Charlotte and Frederick to discuss any of the brutality against Jews with their parents. For one, Margarete supported the Third Reich and Hitler, and she was silent about what was happening to Jewish people. And it simply wasn't part of the culture for adults to discuss politics with children, particularly when absolute obedience to Hitler was mandatory. "You wouldn't dare say a word," said

Charlotte, no matter how much she and Frederick objected internally to what was happening. The climate in Nazi Germany was fraught with paranoia and fear. The Third Reich petrified Germans, and to ensure one's own safety, everyone went along with whatever Hitler said. And the fact was that many Germans, like Margarete and Karl, felt a great sense of pride with Hitler as their leader. He represented power, force, and German dominance, attributes that German citizens hadn't experienced in years.

Frederick did have an opinion about German nationalism, however. On one hand, he, like his father, was apolitical and had no interest in government. But unlike Karl, Frederick wasn't a diehard patriot longing to wear a military uniform for his country. He didn't put on any airs or walk around repeating inflammatory rhetoric. That was not his nature.

He was in the Hitler Youth, along with his sister, Charlotte, because participation was mandatory for anyone with children who wanted to avoid scrutiny or be accused of disrespecting Hitler and Germany. "After school you had to go to meetings from seven to nine, singing songs," said Charlotte. "We all greeted each other with 'Heil Hitler.' We had to everywhere, on the street, in stores, 'Heil Hitler, Heil Hitler!' " Frederick said "Heil Hitler" too, because that was expected of him and he really had no choice. The times in which they lived required 100 percent compliance, and Karl and Margarete wouldn't have allowed any dissent in their household.

However, in 1939, when Hitler invaded Poland, Karl would finally reveal, in a strategic and unassuming way, an objection to what was happening around him. He received orders to leave his family in Vienna to assist with the occupation of Poland. He didn't know the details of the assignment before he arrived, but once there, when he realized they were rounding up Jews and shooting them, he asked for an immediate transfer back. Karl was a German nationalist, not a murderer. He had done his duty in the Great War and was a loyal soldier, but what was going on in Poland was entirely different. Though he couldn't openly object, he convinced military leaders in the Wehrmacht that he was far more useful to the war effort by running his company and that the production of materials would be significantly compromised if he weren't back in Vienna overseeing operations. His argument worked, and Karl returned home to resume his business obligations.[10]

Although he didn't have the stomach for brutality, upon Karl's return his relationship with Frederick didn't change. There wasn't a big eureka moment for him after witnessing carnage at the hands of his own government. If there was one realization he should have taken away from his time in Poland, it should have been that he, like his son, was not a bloodthirsty war machine. But the self-reflection never occurred, and Frederick still appeared to Karl as too weak. There wasn't anything Frederick could have done to gain his father's interest. Karl still didn't care about his family beyond providing material necessities. With war declared, instead of spending precious time with his loved ones and making sure they were safe, Karl still spent many nights away to be with his lovers. Weekends, like dinner, were spent as a family of three for the Alberts, not four. Margarete did her best to act as though Karl's behavior had no impact on her life, though the reality was that she was on her own, married to a narcissist, while the country of her birth began to wreak havoc all over Europe.

Frederick eventually joined the Reichsarbeitsdeinst, commonly referred to as RAD, the State Labor Service. Created in July 1934, it was inspired by the many labor organizations that existed in Germany after the country's staggering defeat in World War I. To combat the devastating economic crisis, toward the end of the 1920s many civic, political, and church groups formed independent work camps across Germany to help provide some form of employment for the many ex-servicemen and the huge numbers of unemployed workers. RAD was mandatory for all Germans between the ages of eighteen and twenty-five for six months, and upon completion, they had to serve for two years in the Wehrmacht. The RAD typically repaired roads, constructed dikes, dug ditches on farms, and performed any service that would help the German military.[11]

Frederick also marched, completed rigorous fitness drills, and sang the songs of Germany's superiority and dominance over the world. One of his duties involved working on a farm, and he hated every minute of it. "It was terrible," said Charlotte. "They had to slaughter a pig. The poor pig was screaming." Frederick's other RAD exercises were equally miserable. An initiation of some sort involved him and his fellow comrades going to the seashore, stripping naked, and washing with sand. Frederick saw no point to the exercise except to teach sheer humiliation.[12]

The simple truth was that Frederick wasn't drawn to the rugged activities that Aryan men were supposed to embrace. He wasn't into sports either. If he had to play, he'd choose a position that required the least amount of endurance and physical contact. He didn't live up to the Third Reich's ideal image of a German man who was tall, blond, muscular, strong, and, above all else, aggressive and hypernationalistic.

Frederick, whose blonde hair had browned and who had a slight frame, was a Renaissance man. He was artistic and romantic. He was against the war and Hitler, but he learned to adapt and did what was expected of him, which was still never enough to warrant any attention from his father. Even though Frederick eventually joined the Wehrmacht to fight for Germany, Karl continued to ignore him. It was almost as if there wasn't anything the son could do to gain his father's respect. Frederick turned to his painting. He was gifted in drawing landscapes. He took inspiration from the renowned works of Caspar David Friedrich, and he loved drawing nudes and portraits of good friends. If there was one thing he excelled in, it was art, which also happened to be the very thing Karl couldn't have cared less about.

Before his conscription, Frederick went briefly to the prestigious Academy of Fine Arts in Vienna. It was a bittersweet accomplishment. Frederick's painting ability, in Margarete's eyes, was something to be nurtured, and she was proud of his work, hanging some of his paintings on the walls of the apartment. Karl didn't notice and had no congratulatory words for Frederick when his son was admitted into one of the best art schools in all of Europe. Painting wasn't a respectable profession in his eyes. Frederick's choices were unacceptable to Karl, who viewed his son as a disappointment.

Art wasn't Frederick's only passion. He also loved jazz and had an affinity for the New Orleans sound of several black musicians, including Louis Armstrong and Sidney Bechet. But the only music allowed in Germany was that performed by German musicians. Any music performed by a non-Aryan was forbidden by the Nazis; listening to black American musicians was unconscionable. "Nigger music," as Hitler referred to jazz, "was forbidden," said Charlotte. Anyone who sought it out was doing so at great risk. You could even go to prison if you were caught listening.

Frederick, isolated from his father, was at least getting attention from his mother at times. In family photos, Margarete even appeared enamored with him, her expression one of pure elation as she gazed at him. But it was more than a mother cooing over her son. Margarete favored Frederick over Charlotte and didn't hide it. She talked to him more, smiled more, and complimented him more. It was a hurtful reality for Charlotte, who couldn't seem to garner attention from either parent. Even when she looked at an old family album at the age of ninety-four, Charlotte seemed upset, as if the feelings of neglect and rejection were still raw. "You can see," she said, pointing to a photo of Frederick. "Mother's favorite, and I'm always on the side and superfluous."

Charlotte's daughter, Kristina Brandner, who was born in 1943, during the war, knew her mother's upbringing had been difficult emotionally. "I grew up with my grandparents in Germany after the war," said Kristina. "There was so much jealousy and bad feelings in that house. Frederick and my mother did not have a happy childhood."

As the war intensified, Frederick made one last, determined effort to bond with Karl. He knew his pursuit of art alienated him from his father, and although he wasn't going to give it up, he decided that he could also be a strong German man if that was what it took to have a relationship with his dad. He would fight just like everyone else and make the same sacrifices that every young soldier was making. Nationalism wasn't in his heart, but he loved his father and wanted him in his life, and so he knew he'd have to do something drastic that exhibited boldness, courage, and strength in order to change Karl's low opinion of him. When he was drafted, Frederick made a decision so uncharacteristic that it was hard to believe: he announced he was joining the Luftwaffe to be a paratrooper. What better way to impress his uncommunicative father than to sign up for an extremely dangerous division of the military?

Frederick wanted his father to see that he was a real man capable of taking risks and confronting danger and death. His desire to join one of the most suicidal sectors of the German air force didn't change one aspect of his strained relationship with Karl, however. To think he could suddenly reinvent himself in his father's eyes turned out to be wishful thinking. Karl's lack of acknowledgment must have been a devastating blow to Frederick. He was willing to risk his life not for Hitler or Germany but for his father's elusive approval. And it meant absolutely nothing to Karl.

Margarete, on the other hand, was proud of Frederick. She, more than any other member of the family, was the most vocal nationalist who believed strongly in Germany's empire. That her son was fighting for their country was an honorable thing.

Yet being in Hitler's army was the last thing Frederick wanted for himself, especially knowing his father didn't care. He had no choice but to fight, of course, as imprisonment or death would be the only option if he refused to participate in Germany's military pursuit of world dominance. His heart would never embrace Hitler's carnage, which meant he would never identify as a Nazi. He was simply doing his mandatory duty.

While Frederick was away in basic training, Charlotte, after finishing high school, believed the best way to rid herself of her parents' rejection was to marry. She was stunning and sophisticated and relished the attention she received from men. It was only a matter of time before she was engaged. When one young man in particular, who believed in Hitler's ideology, asked her to marry, she accepted his proposal. That her new husband was a Nazi sympathizer wasn't necessarily an issue for Charlotte. It was a common occurrence to meet Germans who believed all the rhetoric and propaganda. But Charlotte didn't subscribe to those beliefs herself. She was running away from loneliness, and getting married would finally put an end to a life filled with neglect from her parents. Naturally, the marriage didn't last long, and Charlotte divorced her husband shortly after the birth of their daughter, Kristina, who would be given to Karl and Margarete to rear. "My mother was like my grandfather," said Kristina, reflecting on her upbringing. "She wasn't interested in the family." [13]

Meanwhile, Frederick was struggling in the military. If his training was supposed to turn him into an emotionless warrior, the opposite happened. When he left for the service Frederick kept up a friendship with a classmate from art school named Kurt Wilhelm, who would later become a prominent German film director. They exchanged a lively correspondence about art and artistic freedom, and discussed a famous exhibition of "degenerate art" that was controversial at the time because it was by artists who were banned by Hitler because they were not Aryan and had decadent styles. Frederick was careful to tear Kurt's letters into little pieces after reading them, given the subject matter, because he knew they could get him into trouble, but one was found by a sergeant who put the torn pieces together and reported Frederick. He was court-martialed and reduced in rank. He could never be an officer after that incident; his liberal ideas about art prevented that.

The term "degenerate art," coined by the Nazis, was part of a smear campaign against modern art and artists deemed un-German, Jewish, or Communist in nature. Hitler considered degenerate art works that "insult German feeling, or destroy or confuse natural form or simply reveal an absence of adequate manual and artistic skill." In Munich, in 1937, Adolf Ziegler, one of Hitler's favorite painters and head of the Reich Chamber of Visual Arts, organized an exhibit of "degenerate" works of art that the government seized from museums to serve as contrast to the works in the Great German Art Exhibition, a show that was taking place simultaneously. Hitler forcefully said in a speech that Germany was cracking down on cultural disintegration and shaming "the cliques of chatterboxes, dilettantes and art swindlers," who created works that were considered unpatriotic and disrespectful of Aryan ideals.[14]

The exhibit of "degenerate art" was a seductive topic among art connoisseurs such as Frederick. But that he would be so brazen as to discuss the forbidden works while serving in the military proved how out of place he really was.

Everything Frederick loved—jazz, art, liberal ideas—was counter to the ideology of the Third Reich and the nationalistic views of his parents. Yet somehow, this made his desire to be a paratrooper all the more profound.

But Frederick's dreams of becoming a war hero were quickly thwarted. Many years later, he revealed to his children, in sparse detail, that he hadn't served for very long before he was captured in an Italian village trying to flee on a bike with flat tires.

3.

Fighting Hitler
and Jim Crow

DURING ELINOR'S LAST YEAR OF NURSING SCHOOL in 1943, the American military was deeply entrenched in battle with the Axis Powers all over the world: the Germans and Italians in Europe, North Africa, and the Atlantic, and the Japanese in East Asia and the Pacific. There was hardly a person in the United States who wasn't impacted by the war in some way. The very idea of serving in the military to fight Hitler was appealing to anyone young and patriotic, as well as to those in need of the stable income the military provided, which was arguably one reason why black men enlisted. Given that Jim Crow was just as pervasive in the military, the African Americans who joined were volunteering to meet the threat of fascism head-on even though the liberties they fought for weren't extended to them. World War II united Americans across race, class, faith, and ethnicity. More than thirteen million, or 10 percent of the country's population, would serve in some capacity by the end of the war.[1]

Elinor was patriotic, but there was so much more to her enlistment in the Army Nurse Corps. With her beloved father gone, she needed a fresh start far away from Milton—and after nursing school, far from New York too, where social unrest and deep racial tensions were simmering. Although New York had the appearance of being progressive, the city overtly condoned Jim Crow discrimination in the form of segregated hotels, restaurants, performance halls, and movie theaters.

Before her arrival in Arizona, Elinor was living in Harlem, at 508 West 142nd Street. Central Harlem had been overcrowded since the first wave of the Great Migration began during World War I, when blacks from the South sought better living conditions in the North, hoping to escape the persistent racism and domestic terrorism of their daily lives.[2] In New York, they discovered a different form of discrimination that could be just as oppressive and degrading. The neighborhood had undergone a serious demographic transformation by the time Elinor arrived in the 1940s. In 1910, the black population in Central Harlem hovered around 10 percent, while the white population was 90 percent. By 1940 the numbers had reversed and African Americans accounted for 89 percent of Harlem's residents, with whites only 10 percent of the neighborhood's population.[3] When World War II began, Central Harlem alone—which loosely spans from 155th Street to 110th Street north to south, and from Fifth Avenue to St. Nicholas Avenue east to west—was home to 221,900 residents, a small city squeezed into forty-five blocks.

Just a few months after Elinor graduated from nursing school, one particular incident between a white rookie cop and a black veteran triggered riots across Harlem. The episode involved a black woman named Marjorie Polite, who had checked into the Hotel Braddock on 126th Street and Eighth Avenue, not far from the Apollo Theater. A popular destination for black celebrities and musicians in the 1920s and 1930s, the hotel had since declined in stature and in the 1940s was better known for prostitution and was regularly patrolled.

On August 1, 1943, Polite allegedly requested a different room after she found the first one unsatisfactory. After the second one failed to meet her standards, she asked for a refund. As she was leaving, she asked the porter for the $1 tip she claimed to have given him upon checking in. He denied receiving a tip, and the two began to argue. A white police officer named James Collins reportedly intervened and grabbed Polite by the arm. As they struggled in the lobby, a black veteran named Robert Bandy, a guest at the hotel along with his mother, came downstairs and witnessed the altercation. One account of the incident described Bandy striking the officer and Collins shooting Bandy in the shoulder as he tried to flee.

Word quickly spread about the confrontation, infuriating Harlem residents. Some erroneous accounts were of Bandy lying shot and dying. Angry crowds of African Americans—who had been seething with resentment after their veteran sons, husbands, and brothers served in the United States military and returned to a country that still discriminated against them and denied them employment—took to the streets. By the next morning, Harlem looked like a war zone. Multiple shops had been looted and vandalized, and stones had been thrown through storefronts and apartment windows. Thousands of law enforcement officers were deployed to stop the rioting, including 6,600 cops, 8,000 state guardsmen, and some volunteers. It was reported that five African Americans were killed by the police and four hundred blacks sustained injuries. Approximately five hundred black men and women were arrested. Damages in Harlem ran upward of $5 million, which would be the equivalent of $71.4 million today.[4] Elinor's whereabouts during the riots or her opinion of them isn't known. But the display of racial animosity would have been the first time she witnessed racial strife to that degree.

A public health crisis also raged in the neighborhood at the time. Tuberculosis reached epidemic levels in Harlem in the 1920s and 1930s, fueled by overcrowding and fanned by inadequate medical facilities. Harlem residents teamed up with African American newspapers to demand better health care. Black physicians, nurses, and social workers also joined the cause by initiating an active health education campaign. Health officials typically didn't make an epidemic in the black community a public issue unless it had the potential to impact the health of whites. The tuberculosis crisis perpetuated negative stereotypes of racial inferiority. African Americans were seen as susceptible to disease at higher rates because of their "genetic" deficits. It took the persistent efforts of African American activists to counter the stereotypes by explaining and revealing the links between poverty, segregation, and disease that undermined the health of blacks, rather than any connection to genetics or character.[5]

If Elinor had stayed in New York, she'd be living in an environment that was as volatile as it was thrilling. A career in the military, even for black women, came with the hope that in return for an outward display of patriotism, one would be treated as a full citizen of the United States—something that had been denied to the majority of African Americans whose families had been in the country for generations. For Elinor, whose privileged background positioned her to expect a certain standard of treatment from society, the idea of serving in the Nurse Corps carried even greater expectations. In her eyes, she imagined it would be equivalent to having a prestigious job—one that was far more rewarding and lucrative than that of a regular working nurse.

But when she reported for active duty at Fort Huachuca, seventy miles outside of Tucson, Elinor was greeted by a much harsher reality.

The entire base was surrounded by the Huachuca Mountains, just a twenty-minute drive from the Mexican border. The desert dust was a stark contrast to the topography of the urban Northeast that Elinor had grown accustomed to navigating. Everything looked dry and desolate, and walking even a few feet covered her shoes in reddish-brown dirt. The sunsets, however, were stunning, and like nothing she'd seen before. The pink, orange, and lavender hues illuminating the vast sky were a much-needed reminder of the natural beauty that existed in the world.

Nothing in her past could have prepared Elinor for Arizona. It was as though she'd traveled to another planet. According to 1940 census data, there were 23,679 blacks in Boston.[6] In New York City, they totaled 445,844.[7] In Tucson there were 1,678.[8]

Experiencing Jim Crow for the first time was also a shock. The minuscule population of blacks who lived in Arizona was forced to attend segregated schools, and multiple restaurants and hotels refused their patronage, even for blacks in uniform. And the defense plants throughout the state would not hire African Americans, who were also turned away at the polls if they could not read passages from the Constitution, a requirement that white residents did not have to meet in order to vote.[9]

Fort Huachuca consisted of numerous variously sized buildings, some wooden, some brick, some stone, sprawled over miles of wide-open desert. What stood out immediately were the separate facilities for blacks and whites. Many blacks who migrated from the South discovered that the West was just as inhospitable as the regions they had fled. While Boston was certainly not a racial utopia, Milton was progressive enough that Elinor's family was able to interact with whites peacefully, attending the same schools, working at the same jobs, and shopping at the same stores. Now, in the military, she suddenly wasn't fit to be in the same barracks and eating establishments as white people.

The forced separation felt like a punishment. Serving in the U.S. military was supposed to make her feel dignified. Instead, Elinor felt humiliated.

Nowhere on her application to the United States Army Nurse Corps did it describe the segregated facilities she would be expected to inhabit. It also never mentioned anything about being treated like a second-class citizen. Scores of black women like Elinor eagerly arrived at Fort Huachuca with the best of intentions, only to be severely disappointed by their own government.

Between 1943 and 1945 Fort Huachuca was the largest training post for Negro troops, as they were called then, in the United States. The only whites left at Huachuca when Elinor arrived in 1944 were the officers in charge of the blacks in uniform.[10]

The relationship between black enlisted men and white officers was notoriously acrimonious. There were many reported instances of verbal abuse and condescending behavior from white officers toward black soldiers. One particular high-ranking white officer at Fort Huachuca, Major General Edward "Ned" Almond, was known for humiliating black enlisted men. Almond was vocal in his opinion that blacks didn't make strong leaders and that troops of black men were successful only if white men led them. Under no circumstances would he allow any white military men to be under the command of a black officer.[11] Almond was known to openly disparage the quality and performance of black soldiers, called them "boys," and unapologetically stated that blacks were inferior to whites.

Many of the black soldiers were from urban areas such as Detroit, Cleveland, Chicago, and New York. They were drafted at higher numbers than southern black men, who could be given exemptions from military service if plantation owners convinced local draft boards that they were needed to pick cotton, a staple in the war effort, since it was used in airplane tires and also to make military uniforms.[12]

For African Americans raised in the bustling cities of the North, Arizona was bleak, unaccommodating, and depressing. Even if their urban neighborhoods were overpopulated and impoverished, there were businesses they could patronize, including mom-and-pop stores, hotels, barbershops, hair salons, soda counters, and nightclubs. But Fort Huachuca and the surrounding small towns respected Jim Crow, excluding African Americans by means of segregation. Even on base, there were two separate hospitals for blacks and whites, two sets of civilian quarters for the local residents who lived and worked there, two service clubs for military personnel of any rank, and, most glaringly, two separate officers' clubs.[13]

An inspector general's report in August 1942 highlighted the problems with the segregated facilities at Fort Huachuca and the morale issues they caused. The report noted that Jim

Crow policies directly impacted the performance of black enlisted men.

The morale of the black soldiers set the tone for the black nurses who were stationed at the base. African Americans were accustomed to being treated differently because of their skin color, but it was nonetheless surprising to black nurses that their own military would isolate them, particularly when nursing shortages would be an ongoing dilemma throughout the war.

Black women wanted to be nurses long before World War II. Aside from teaching, nursing was the only professional career available to African American women after the Civil War. The first black woman to work as a professionally trained nurse in the United States was Mary Eliza Mahoney, who earned a diploma from the New England Hospital for Women and Children in 1879. The hospital was founded in 1862 and stipulated in its charter that only "one Negro and one Jew" would be accepted as students each year. Given this school was located in the Northeast and considered progressive in its policies, the situation for southern African American women who wanted to be nurses was almost hopeless.[14]

The dire health care conditions for southern blacks caught the attention of white philanthropists. In particular, John D. Rockefeller and his wife, Laura Spelman Rockefeller, whose family had deep roots in the antislavery movement, decided to finance a southern institution for black women, the Atlanta Baptist Female Seminary, founded in

1881 and later renamed Spelman College. The Rockefellers funded a nurse-training department in 1886, but the program was dissolved in 1927 given the limited resources of the small campus hospital, MacVicar, and because Spelman had since become a liberal arts institution.[15] But a string of nursing programs at black hospitals and historically black colleges and universities were subsequently created, including the Dixie Hospital Training School in Hampton, Virginia, in 1891, the Tuskegee Institute nursing training course in 1892, and the Freedmen's Hospital Nursing School in Washington D.C. in 1894. By the mid-1920s, more than twenty-five new nursing schools had been established, along with two hundred black hospitals, in the South, Midwest, and Northeast. Most of these institutions were privately owned and were funded by white philanthropists.[16]

Despite the emergence of black nursing schools, access to health care for African Americans in the South remained quite limited. The 1896 landmark Supreme Court case *Plessy v. Ferguson*, which legalized the doctrine of separate but equal, had a devastating effect on blacks. Although the Supreme Court mandated equal facilities, states rarely cooperated. Blacks were excluded from publicly supported municipal hospitals, and black doctors were denied access to internships, residencies, and hospital staff appointments. The consequences of these segregationist policies included high morbidity and mortality rates in black communities.[17]

As more black women became nurses in the early 1900s, there was a growing interest among them in joining the U.S.

Army Nurse Corps. But they were not successful because they lacked the necessary medical affiliations the military required, which were granted solely by the American Nursing Association, an organization that mostly excluded black women. In response, a black nurse named Adah Thoms cofounded with Mary Eliza Mahoney the National Association of Colored Graduate Nurses (NACGN) in 1908. Their main purpose was to provide black registered nurses (RNs) with an accredited organization that would advocate on their behalf for hospital staff jobs, professional nursing associations, and military enlistments.

After the United States declared war on Germany in 1917, African American nurses tried to enroll in the Red Cross, since that was the procurement agency for the Army Nurse Corps. They were all rejected because they weren't members of the American Nursing Association, which wouldn't admit them. Every door seemed to be closed. Thoms began a lively correspondence with Jane Delano, chair of the Red Cross, to explain the impossible position black nurses were in: all of the army's required memberships involved organizations that discriminated against African Americans. After a back-and-forth about the challenges that black nurses faced despite their qualifications, Delano approached the surgeon general of the U.S. Army about the situation. The army had the final say on the enrollment of African American nurses, and the answer given was no.

A health crisis in 1918 inadvertently opened the door. The flu pandemic that year required a constant supply of replacement nurses, which persuaded the surgeon general to finally authorize the use of a handful of black nurses in World War I. That seemed like a major accomplishment to African American nurses at the time, and the NACGN assumed they had made official inroads into the military.[18]

A year after Hitler invaded Poland in 1939 the United States began an aggressive war preparedness program. The U.S. Army Nurse Corps knew the war would require more nurses, and they set out to expand their recruiting services. Black nurses became energized by the urgent calls from Congress, local leaders, and media outlets encouraging nurses to join the army. The NACGN alerted its membership to enroll in the Red Cross, still a required affiliation for enlistment in the nurse corps, but once again black nurses faced a serious problem.[19] African American nurses from fifteen southern states still could not join the American Nurses Association, which was a qualification to enroll in the Red Cross. Nothing had changed in twenty years. The U.S. Army still did not want black nurses to serve. Even black nurses in the North who were able to join the Red Cross were rejected, receiving a letter that read: "Your application for appointment to the Army Nurse Corps cannot be given favorable consideration as there are no provisions in Army regulations for the appointment of colored nurses in the Corps."[20]

Elinor would not have been able to enlist when she did if someone hadn't challenged the army, and the NACGN couldn't have chosen a better leader to take on the task than a stout, bespectacled West Indian woman named Mabel Staupers.

Born in Barbados in 1890, Mabel Keaton Staupers received her nursing degree from the Freedmen's Hospital School of Nursing in Washington, D.C. Although she started off as a private nurse, Staupers would establish herself as a leading medical professional specializing in the recruitment of black nurses for various hospital staffing and teaching positions across the country. She was so diligent at her job that African American physicians contacted her directly to request nurses for various employment opportunities.

She was a mastermind at networking and coalition building, and her efforts were especially noticed by the National Association of Colored Graduate Nurses, and after working fifteen years in Washington, D.C., and Philadelphia, Staupers headed to New York to be the NACGN's new executive secretary in 1934.[21]

Staupers was well aware of the American Nurses Association's refusal to admit black nurses in their southern chapters. But she helped pressure the Red Cross to make an exception for southern black nurses who were members of the NACGN and who met all the other qualifications. Her real goal was to make sure black nurses received the same opportunities as white nurses, particularly in serving the military.

The rejection letters from the U.S. Army Nurse Corps enraged Staupers. The curriculum at black nursing schools was comparable to the curriculum at nursing schools that admitted only whites, so it was clear that racism was driving the military's decision. The fact that the American government would try to fight a war against fascism while subjecting its own citizens to racism was not lost on Staupers, who had a solid relationship with the top civil rights organizations, including the NAACP and the National Council of Negro Women. She decided that African American nurses deserved to be treated far better, and in 1940 she decided to directly confront the powers that be, Surgeon General of the Army James Magee.

Staupers mobilized an army of supporters, including the NAACP, civil rights activist Mary McLeod Bethune, black newspapers, white philanthropists, Congresswoman Frances Bolton, who was a longtime supporter of nurses, and First Lady Eleanor Roosevelt. Staupers even sent telegrams to President Franklin D. Roosevelt, which she would do until his death, urging him to allow black nurses to serve their country and "give Negro nurses the opportunity for full service as American citizens."[22] There wasn't a door she didn't knock on in an attempt to gain support and momentum for her cause.

Magee was a decorated surgeon and army man, and a veteran of the Great War.[23] He was also known to be a staunch segregationist. On March 7, 1941, Magee met with a special health council for blacks that included Staupers, who insisted on the elimination of race-based restrictions on joining the Army Nurse Corps. The pressure continued beyond the meeting until Magee finally acquiesced, and the

U.S. Army Nurse Corps accepted fifty-six black nurses in April 1941. But the admittance of black nurses came with a restricted quota and a continuation of segregation. "Negro nurses and other Negro professional personnel would only be called to serve in hospitals or wards devoted exclusively to the treatment of Negro soldiers," said Magee, who emphasized that separate units were consistent with the racial policies and customs that American culture had adopted long before, and that black nurses could take it or leave it.

Undeterred, Mabel Staupers accepted the offer but kept pushing for racial inclusion in the army. Out of the initial group of fifty-six nurses, all were sent to segregated bases: half went to Fort Bragg, North Carolina, and the other half to Camp Livingston, Louisiana. In 1942, sixty nurses were sent to Fort Huachuca.[24]

Elinor's training didn't begin on a good note. Hot, sweaty, and covered in grime, she stood silently in formation while one of the commanding officers announced that the uniforms hadn't arrived yet, so for basic training the nurses would have to wear whatever they had brought. This meant they would have to complete their prerequisites and drills wearing either the clothes on their backs or the nursing school whites they had packed. The reason given for the delay was that the military uniforms were changing and there weren't enough new ones to distribute. "Others said it was because the 'black' army always got what was left," recalled Elinor years later.[25]

It was a blow to the nurses' integrity—wearing civilian

clothing for basic training at a military base located in the blazing hot desert. Part of the rank and prestige of representing the United States during wartime was wearing a military uniform. Elinor had already filled a scrapbook with photos of her in nursing school wearing her pristine white jacket-and-skirt ensembles. Now she would be running around a dusty base, drenched in sweat, wearing clothes from home. The army could have allowed the nurses to train in older uniforms until the new ones arrived—anything was better than nothing—but Elinor, along with her fellow nursing sisters, would quickly find out that they, as black women, would come last in every situation.

Six months after Pearl Harbor, there were twelve thousand nurses on active duty in the U.S. Army Nurse Corps. Very few had any military experience, and the majority were largely ignorant of the army way of life. It took until 1943 for Lieutenant General Brehon B. Somerville, commanding general of the Army Service Forces, to authorize a structured, mandatory four-week training course for all newly commissioned army nurses. On July 15, 1944, the same day Elinor's army acceptance letter was issued, the War Department established the first basic training center for black army nurses at Fort Huachuca, located in the fort's segregated black hospital, referred to as Hospital One. Elinor's basic training included lessons in field sanitation, military protocol, and defense against air and chemical strikes, as well as a monotonous crash course in the skills they had learned in nursing school: administering prescriptions, taking X-rays, surgery prep, bedside care, and filing charts.[26]

The living conditions at Fort Huachuca were Spartan. Elinor wasn't expecting stately furnishings, but none of the nurses were prepared for the depressing appearance of the barracks. They were long wooden shotgun houses painted beige, sitting on a mixture of gravel and dirt, each divided into small bedrooms with one common lounge area where the nurses could talk and play bridge or bid whist. Living on a military base would take some getting used to for anyone, but for black nurses from the North, like Elinor, the experience of entering buildings for "colored" people was infuriating. Many of the other nurses at Fort Huachuca came from the South. These women were used to Jim Crow. Overt discrimination was all they had ever known. But how was Elinor supposed to go from sitting wherever she wanted in a restaurant to socializing in the officers' club for Negroes?

Basic training lasted for several weeks, so there really was no other choice but for Elinor to accept her new environment. She had made the decision to join, and she needed to see it through. From the very beginning, though, a bitterness began to brew inside her that would grow with each passing day.

There were hardly any places outside of Fort Huachuca that would serve a black person. Uniform or not, businesses and restaurants would deny service to African Americans. The poor treatment of black nurses, however, wasn't nearly as bad as what black soldiers faced.

Complaints from soldiers who wrote home from bases across the country about the terrible racist conditions they encountered initially fell on deaf ears. But the steady flow of heartbreaking letters that wives, girlfriends, siblings, and parents received month after month created such concern that it was only a matter of time before the NAACP and the Negro press got involved.[27]

Fort Huachuca was home to as many as twenty thousand black soldiers at a time, and the commanding general and his staff didn't seem very interested in keeping their morale high. One black soldier, Sergeant Carter from the 597th Field Artillery Battalion, recalled, "Here was a big sprawling camp containing between 17,000 and 20,000 black men with a small percentage of white officers . . . who enforced the strictest segregation possible between themselves and the black officers. Their only contact was strictly in relation to military activities; social contact was out. How they could possibly function together in combat was a question that had to pass through many a black officer's minds, not to mention the minds of enlisted men."[28]

The black medical staff at Fort Huachuca had the largest group of African American medical professionals in the military. Hospital One, the first all-black hospital at the base, had 946 beds and was designated exclusively for blacks, from patients to personnel. It was led by Lieutenant Colonel Midian Othello Bousefield, the highest-ranking African American army physician. There were three dental clinics, with dentists treating approximately a thousand cases per week. The medical corps was staffed with forty-two black medical officers and many African American orderlies. In 1942, there were sixty black nurses, and by 1943, there were a hundred. The number grew each year as Fort Huachuca became the transitional station to train black nurses before shipping them out to various posts throughout the country and occasionally overseas.[29]

With an elite group of medical professionals and an abundance of black enlisted men in the immediate vicinity, Elinor and the other nurses primarily socialized inside the gates of Fort Huachuca. There wasn't anywhere else to go, and at least when they stayed on base, they were surrounded by other black people who acknowledged and appreciated them. The 25th and 368th Infantries, the largest units of black troops, were activated at the fort; they included the fabled 92nd and 93rd Divisions, which had helped France achieve victory during World War I.[30] There were thousands of black military personnel everywhere on base, which made both the black nurses and soldiers happy. Seeing black men in uniforms smiling and tipping their hats was comforting, and more in line with what a young nurse like Elinor thought the army would be like.

The concentrated population of young black women and men at Fort Huachuca had distinct social advantages. In 1942 two black companies of the Women's Auxiliary Army Corps (later simplified to WAC) arrived to assist with various jobs around the base. These women were part of the Service Command, whose tasks ranged from repairing stalled trucks to putting on dances for the troops—anything to boost morale and aid the war effort.[31] That same year, Fort Huachuca finally built an officers' club for African Americans, called Mountain View.

When Elinor arrived in 1944, Mountain View had been in operation for two years as an upscale social destination for high-ranking African American military personnel who were not allowed at Lake Side, Fort Huachuca's officers' club for whites. Before Mountain View's completion, while white officers smoked cigars, drank beer, listened to music and danced with female personnel or their wives, black officers with the same rank had nowhere comparable to congregate and pass the time. They couldn't even frequent the establishments in the local town. At Mountain View, black officers could finally socialize with dignity.

Whenever there were entertainers or major celebrities visiting Fort Huachuca to entertain the troops, such as Lena Horne or Count Basie, however, whites were in front and blacks sat in the back, regardless of rank. On one occasion when Lena Horne was performing, she stepped down from the stage and walked to the back to face the black soldiers. She reportedly said, "I came here to sing for the colored troops. They're back here." Horne had a similar experience at Fort Robinson in Arkansas in early 1945. The first show was for the white troops. The second show was for black troops.[32]

As the demographics of Fort Huachuca began to shift, with many white enlisted men and officers transferred elsewhere, the remaining white officers were outnumbered by African American officers and enlisted men—a fact that fueled an ongoing visceral tension between the two racial groups. Because of the black-white ratio, Fort Huachuca, in the opinion of some of the white officers, was a less prestigious base because they associated blacks with deficient performance and ability. As their white counterparts were transferred out, the white officers remaining felt they were among a subpar population, and they made that clear.[33]

Consequently, the ratio of white officers to black enlisted men spawned a need for each group to diminish the other. Whites, who were fewer in number, used their race to disparage blacks. And blacks, in response, criticized the capabilities and stature of the white officers in charge. One lieutenant from the 93rd Division who was reinstated on the base in 1942 recalled the animosity that permeated life at Fort Huachuca:

> Ninety-five to ninety-eight percent of the white officers were southerners. I think I was in a position to say that the majority of the white officers with the 93d were people who could not have made it with the 37th or 87th divisions, or any white division of any caliber. They might have been all right in the quartermasters, or some laundry units. Instead of being sent to jobs they were fit for, they were sloughed off on the 93d. . . . The black officers as a whole were superior to their senior officers in the 93d. And the black officers knew it; dissension was bound to

arise. Then too, those white officers, though Lord knows they would never admit it, knew they were outclassed by their junior officers and this heightened their resentment. They took advantage of their rank to strike out at black officers.[34]

Even the presence of a superstar proved to do little for race relations between blacks and whites at Fort Huachuca. Boxer Joe Louis, born in rural and impoverished Alabama to sharecroppers, became the heavyweight champion of the world when he knocked out James Braddock on June 22, 1937. Louis became a hero to all soldiers, white and black, when in 1942, after defeating Buddy Baer, he donated his share of the purse to the Army and Navy Relief Fund. When Louis himself enlisted in the army and became a sergeant, he visited Fort Huachuca in 1943 to stage an exhibition match for the soldiers.[35] It was a highlight among black and white soldiers alike. But the racism continued.

And the incidents of discrimination inevitably affected the plight of black nurses. After gaining admittance in 1941, the actual enlistment of black nurses in the army remained incredibly low. It was obvious the army didn't want them in the war effort. In 1944, there were only 330 black nurses in the U.S. Army Nurse Corps, even though 8,000 had tried to enlist.[36]

After Elinor and the other nurses in her cohort completed basic training in the summer of 1944, the army gave them official orders to report to another destination as second lieutenants in the U.S. Army Nurse Corps. Until then, none of the nurses knew where they would end up during the war. Many longed to go overseas. There was a group of black nurses from the 25th Infantry who were in New Guinea and the Philippines tending to the black soldiers stationed in the Pacific. But foreign assignments were rare for black nurses and largely depended on how many black soldiers would be stationed nearby. There was a revolving door of transfers at Fort Huachuca. Soldiers came in and were then deployed out to other bases. Black nurses tended to follow the black soldiers, given the strict segregation rules, but Elinor's group received shocking instructions. They were headed to Camp Florence, a prisoner-of-war camp for German soldiers located in an even more remote area of Arizona.

Questioning orders was not part of military protocol, but the black nurses wondered among themselves why they were being sent to treat Germans instead of American soldiers. Why were Germans even in the United States when the war was being fought overseas? None of it made any sense. Being told to care for the enemy was unfathomable. Their question was partly answered when they were brought together by the commanding officer, who told them that black nurses were being shipped to POW camps because there had been too much fraternization between the POWs and the white nurses who were stationed at those facilities.[37]

The news angered Elinor and her peers. Some wrote to Mabel Staupers and the NAACP to complain about the POW assignment. Would they be in danger caring for Nazis? These were the very people who thought nonwhites were subhuman. Why should African American nurses be exposed to such a potentially volatile group of people? They could barely handle the discrimination they faced from their fellow American citizens. The assignment also seemed counterintuitive to Jim Crow laws. If blacks weren't supposed to be in contact with whites, then it didn't make sense for black nurses to treat German soldiers. The sad truth was that the military had a quota system that didn't allow for a substantial number of black nurses to participate in the war effort. It didn't matter that there was a serious nursing shortage. A decision had been made that black nurses were to be utilized strictly for the care of black troops or POWs. White nurses were shipped out whenever possible to care exclusively for Allied soldiers. And though white nurses would have to care for a substantial number of prisoners of war throughout World War II, whenever there was an opportunity to replace white nurses in POW camps with black ones, the swap was made. Either the U.S. military thought there would be no risk of fraternization between Germans and black nurses or it didn't even care enough to be concerned. However insulting these assumptions, there was nothing Elinor could do to protest her assignment. Black nurses, from the start, were not a welcomed group, and the army expressed this rationale explicitly.

With her new khaki-colored Army Nurse Corps uniform, which had finally arrived, she boarded a train for the two-hour trip to Camp Florence, where the staff consisted of white guards, white military police (MPs), white doctors, and a handful of white nurses they'd be replacing. The reality of Elinor's situation was grim. If she hadn't realized it at the start of basic training, she certainly did when she arrived at the POW camp. She was defending her country's freedom at the expense of her own.

4.

German POWs in the United States

In 1944, Gladys Powell was a widow at 48, living alone in Milton, in poor health and suffering from hypertension, the same condition that had contributed to her husband's death a year earlier. The former no-nonsense southern belle didn't have her daughters nearby; they had all started new chapters of their lives in other parts of the country. Gladys was in the Red Cross in Arizona; Elinor was in the U.S. Army Nurse Corps, also stationed in Arizona; and the youngest, Ruth, was a student at Howard University in Washington, D.C.

The Powells were hardly the only family to be separated and scattered as a result of the war. The workforce was transformed as people left their jobs to serve in the military, leaving dozens of industries inadequately staffed, and the devastatingly large number of casualties resulted in broken families in addition to vacant jobs.

The staggering numbers of men and women entering the armed services triggered fundamental shifts in the American workforce. The number of men in the army more than quadrupled between 1941 and 1943, from 1.5 million to 6.9 million. By 1945, the total number in the army jumped to 8.3 million. Out of that number, 73 percent served overseas, spending an average of sixteen months abroad. By the end of World War II, more than 12 million Americans served in the U.S. Army, Navy, Marines, and Coast Guard combined.[1]

Farms, factories, plants, and canneries had to figure out a way to cope with the sudden lack of manpower. In particular, cotton farmers needed pickers. Cotton was a crop that wasn't managed by agricultural machinery yet; cotton picking required backbreaking manual labor in order to extract the cotton from the thorny bush. Cotton was vital to the war effort, but demands for it had begun much earlier. Besides clothing and linens, cotton had been used since the early twentieth century to make rubber tires and airplane wing covers. In Arizona, it had become a substantial cash crop, central to the state's economy. Several tire companies had moved there, including Goodyear Tire and Rubber Company, which set up factories in 1917 in a town later named in its honor. By 1920, there were 800,000 acres of cotton in Arizona.[2] After the Great War, the cotton boom ended—until the coveted fabric was needed again for World War II. When American men continued to enlist, leaving the work of sharecropping (and particularly picking cotton) unattended, the U.S. military took advantage of another source of cheap labor: prisoners of war.

The transfer of hundreds of thousands of Axis prisoners of war to American soil is one of the great untold stories of World War II. There were 371,683 German POWs, 51,156 Italians, and 5,413 Japanese detained in the United States during World War II in more than six hundred camps scattered across the country.[3] Having this many foreign prisoners of war interned within its borders was a new experience for the United States. It was a moment in history that would not be as widely reported or emphasized for future generations to absorb.[4]

In Europe, where cities were constantly being bombed or occupied militarily, there wasn't adequate space for Allied forces to imprison all of the German and Italian POWs. Britain had been capturing and housing German soldiers without any relief before the United States declared war after Pearl Harbor in 1941, and the situation was approaching crisis mode.

Initially, the United States was reluctant to make an agreement with Britain to take in prisoners of war. Despite outside appearances of congeniality, the two countries had different philosophies and strategies about the direction of the war. The rocky relationship made the United States hesitant to partner with Britain on the POW situation, and the United States resisted absorbing POWs for as long as possible in spite of persistent pressure from Britain.[5] Security problems were another concern raised by the prospect of having Nazi prisoners on U.S. soil. FBI director J. Edgar Hoover, paranoid about the possibility of German POWs escaping and wreaking havoc on American society, reportedly said of the typical Wehrmacht soldier, "Trained as he is in the technique of destruction, he is a danger to our internal security, our war production, and the lives and safety of our citizens." [6]

But the United States acquiesced, agreeing in August 1942 to take in fifty thousand prisoners of war, even though there wasn't a precise plan in place for what to do with them initially.[7]

The POWs would be working in camps, a provision approved under the terms of the Geneva Convention of 1929. The treaty essentially protected captured soldiers from inhumane treatment, but, depending on their rank, prisoners could still be forced to work for their captors. In the United States, the majority of enlisted German POWs worked for the U.S. Army on its military installations, but many were also contracted out to work for civilian employers. Noncommissioned officers were given supervisory work, while commissioned officers weren't required to work at all, although they could volunteer to do so.[8]

Prisoners of war were a boost to the wartime economy. If some were willing to assist in American intelligence gathering by divulging Nazi military information, then the arrangement was even more beneficial. But the United States had never before detained tens of thousands of enemy combatants at one time, and the experience proved immensely challenging. Some German prisoners of war had been detained in the United States during the Great War, but the number was much smaller, and that experience was not remotely reflective of what the country faced in the 1940s.[9]

From the start, prisoner of war camps were primarily located in the rural South. Eventually camps were erected all over the United States, but building costs in the South were particularly low, and southern farmers had an ongoing need for dependable and cheap unskilled labor.[10]

Some of the labor needs were specific to the region. In the Appalachian areas and northern Minnesota and Michigan, thousands of POWs were used for logging and lumbering. In Arkansas, they picked grapes; and in New York State and Northern Illinois they worked in canning plants for the food services industry.[11] In Arizona, the need, of course, was for cotton picking—a task German and Italian POWs would quickly come to loathe.

Cotton picking had traditionally been the hardest work, reserved for the poorest people. During the Great Depression, 400,000 Mexican cotton pickers were deported after a nativist movement among white residents forced them out. The cotton still needed to be harvested, though, and cotton farmers recruited migrants from what were referred to as dust bowl states—the Texas Panhandle, Oklahoma, New Mexico, Colorado, and Kansas, where farmland had been destroyed by overuse that left it susceptible to erosion by devastating winds, producing dust storms that forced families to flee and become migrant workers. But after a few years of harvesting cotton in Arizona, the migrant workers had moved on, finding less strenuous and better-paying employment opportunities in the defense industries, and the cotton farmers needed help again. They appealed to the U.S. government, and the POWs became the solution.[12]

Many German POWs were captured in Italy, and Frederick seems to have been one of them, although even his family has a complicated relationship to his wartime story. "My father didn't talk about his experience," said his son Chris Albert. The only story the Albert children received was the brief one Frederick shared with them—he had been a paratrooper and was caught in an Italian village while trying to escape from the Allies on a bike with flat tires.

His military papers, which Chris found decades after the war, included a prisoner of war registration card with Frederick's POW number: 81G-244-649. The United States assigned serial numbers to each captured soldier that indicated the soldier's nationality and place of capture. Interestingly, and unbeknownst to his family, Frederick's serial number indicated that he had been captured in North Africa.[13]

On the same card, Frederick's position in the German military was listed as "SAN. SOLD" and his division as "LW SAN.G. 1/1," which seems to indicate that he was a low-ranking medical soldier in the Luftwaffe. Of course, errors were made in paperwork all the time, but it's unlikely that a paratrooper would be listed incorrectly as a medic. The most reasonable explanation was that in an attempt to impress his children, Frederick told them that he was an elite paratrooper. Perhaps he still longed to be the hard-core military hero he had wanted to be in his father's eyes.[14]

In all likelihood, Frederick's unit was en route to Africa, but he just never made it there. In 1942, the United States began a lengthy surge in northern Africa against the Axis powers. More than 100,000 soldiers under the leadership of Generals George Patton and Omar Bradley joined forces with British troops led by General Bernard Montgomery to wage intense battles against German troops under General Erwin Rommel along the Mediterranean coast of Africa, comprising Algeria, Libya, and Tunisia. The casualties were extensive, thousands of men died, and several thousand German soldiers were taken prisoner.[15]

Germans captured in Africa were first detained in make-shift processing camps hastily erected by Allied forces in places such as Marrakesh, Casablanca, and other North African cities and towns. Soldiers captured in Europe, as Frederick said he was, were detained primarily in France and England. The seriously wounded were transported to hospitals. Other prisoners were held there just long enough to receive a medical examination, get inoculated and deloused, be stripped of their possessions, and then be processed and assigned a serial number before being put on a ship for the transatlantic journey to the United States. Prisoners also had to complete a form that required fingerprints and a medical history; the form was sent to the International Red Cross and Swiss authorities so that their families could be informed about the status of their loved ones.[16]

Frederick must have been detained for a few weeks in one of the transitional camps. Karl and Margarete Albert didn't know where he was, nor did his sister, Charlotte. When he joined the Luftwaffe, Frederick lost contact with his family. At some point, when the bombings in Austria intensified, the Alberts temporarily left Vienna, so for a time Frederick didn't know how to reach them either.

Although Frederick had no way to know how long he would be in the transitional camp or where he would be headed for the duration of his captivity, his proficiency in English was an asset. At least he was able to listen to his American captors and pick up clues from time to time.

Language barriers were one of the biggest hurdles in processing German POWs, not only in North Africa and Europe but in the United States as well. The Americans quickly found out that not only could many of the POWs not speak English, some of them couldn't speak German either. Wehrmacht POWs included soldiers from Lithuania, Estonia, Poland, Hungary, Serbia, and Finland who couldn't speak any more German than their American captors.[17] The situation reflected Hitler's desperation to recruit as many fighters as possible, even those who weren't part of his idealized German race.

To make for an even more confusing and haphazard process, hardly any American translators worked at the makeshift POW camps, because of the high demand for German and Italian translators needed for intelligence gathering, radio transmission, and interrogation of high-ranking Axis officials. It didn't take long for German prisoners to figure out that the language barrier could work in their favor.

The clerk-typists who were functioning without translators recorded POWs' personal information as best they could. But some prisoners tricked them by providing false names and inaccurate ranks. In the United States, the problem was even more severe. Some camps had a single interpreter for more than eight thousand prisoners.[18]

Margarete, Karl, and Charlotte were eventually notified by the International Red Cross that Frederick had been captured in Italy and taken as a prisoner of war by the Americans, but that was all the information they were given. In the meantime, Frederick had been put aboard a massive destroyer bound for the United States. Ships of this kind were known to have thousands of prisoners on board, confined mostly to spaces belowdecks, sleeping in five-tiered bunks or three-tiered hammocks.[19] The amount of time the POWs were allowed to stay on deck varied depending on the temperament of the military police on guard. Some POWs were allowed only thirty minutes a day above deck for fresh air and a cigarette break, while others reported getting a few hours. The prisoners had no idea where they were headed, and none of the guards, armed with shotguns but surprisingly friendly, told them anything, except one, who answered "the desert" when asked, which the prisoners took to be a joke. In the barracks below, the POWs played out every scenario imagined, some actually relieved that the fighting was over for them. But many were uncertain of their fate. Would they be hanged? Imprisoned in inhumane conditions? Interrogated and beaten regularly if they didn't

divulge German military secrets? A great many of the soldiers had been conscripted into the Wehrmacht; they fought
because they had to, not because they necessarily agreed
with Hitler's brutality. Soldiers regularly suffered from anxiety attacks, in addition to persistent nausea and the chronic
intestinal viruses that plagued large numbers of men in
combat. The quality of the food on the transatlantic voyage
did mitigate some of their fears, however. They ate T-bone
steaks, ice cream, and grapefruit.[20] But it seemed too good
to be true under the circumstances. Skeptical prisoners were
convinced something bad was going to happen soon.

Finally arriving at shipping docks on the eastern seaboard
in Boston and New York—though some destroyers docked
in Virginia and Louisiana—Frederick and the other prisoners, as soon as they stepped off the ship, listened to an American interpreter explain their rights as captured military
personnel in enemy hands—all the provisions established in
the 1929 Geneva Convention Relative to the Treatment of
Prisoners of War.[21] Before they boarded trains to their final
destinations, the prisoners were deloused again, usually by
black servicemen.

For many German POWs, their first interaction with
African Americans took place during the war. The drivers
of the trucks used to transport captured German soldiers to
camps in Northern Africa and Europe were usually African
American men, and that task also came with the responsibility of protecting the POWs from any mob attacks by angry civilians who tried to rush the vehicles and throw rocks.

In fact, an unlikely bond between black American soldiers and German POWs sometimes developed because blacks knew from their own experiences in the United States what it felt like to be the target of civilian mob violence.

The protectiveness of blacks bewildered the POWs at first. A German prisoner recalled a time when black soldiers protected POWs from an angry mob in France. "Had they not acted so vigorously, we would have fared quite badly. On this occasion we experienced for the first time how much compassion the colored Americans had for us. We were only able to solve this mystery after having our experiences with them in America." [22]

German prisoners immediately remarked on the entrenched racial hierarchy in the United States. Some remembered African American men wearing pristine white jackets serving them during their days-long train journey to the camps. The black attendants brought food and drinks to the POWs at their seats, and stayed on call the entire trip while the Germans slept. They even called the prisoners "sir." [23] It was startling to witness such deference by Americans considering that Germans were technically enemies, not to mention prisoners of war who might well have killed Americans in combat. But it was an authentic picture of how the United States regarded its black citizens and the inherent expectation of subservience to whites, even if they were Nazis. Overall, the prisoners were surprised at how mannered the Americans of both races were toward them upon arrival. POW Karl-Heinz Hackbarth was astounded

by the comfortable accommodations en route to his assigned camp, Fort Custer near Battle Creek, Michigan. "We
couldn't believe we were allowed to sit in upright seats on
a Pullman car. There were a couple of guards in the front
and back of each car. If you had to use the bathroom, you
had to raise your hand, and a guard would escort you."[24]
There were also stories from German POWs that were less
than flattering about the transport. Some prisoners reportedly found the trips "brutalizing," with packed train cars
and harsh orders that barely allowed them to move on the
hours-long journeys. More serious allegations surfaced
about sick POWs who died en route and were thrown over-
board, but these claims were never substantiated.[25]

The train journey across the American terrain would be
most of the German POWs' first experience of the United
States. The temperature in the Pullman cars that Frederick
rode in soared as the train ride grew longer. The 100-degree
weather of the Deep South was unlike anything they had
ever experienced. As the trains headed to camps on the
West Coast, the conversations among the prisoners halted
when they passed through Texas and the military bases with
rows of B-17 bombers, known as Flying Fortresses, came
into full view. These were the planes that the POWs knew
were destined to obliterate their cities, homes, and families.
There was nothing they could do except hope that the war
would end before the bombs touched the ground.[26]

The picturesque trips through the United States surprised
many of the men, who had been led to believe that America

had been bombed by the Luftwaffe—one of the numerous lies Hitler's propaganda machine had peddled to the German people throughout the war. Some of the POWs weren't quite ready to accept that Hitler had deceived them; others felt that being captured toward the end of the war was a relief.[27]

The dramatic entrance to Camp Florence was set against the desert landscape that backed up to the Superstition Mountains, to the east of Phoenix. As the incoming train began its slow approach, the POWs saw a large sign that said "Florence" made of stones, flanked by a big letter "F" painted white on a nearby hillside.

Camp Florence was a campus of separate buildings built in 1942. It was dry, desolate, and without any green space until its POW population became large enough to participate in a lawn-building project. Prisoners shoveled, removed dense dirt to build low dikes for irrigation, and planted grass seed in the moist adobe soil. Having grass and a bit of color helped with morale in the otherwise somber, dusty, and remote camp.[28]

The residents of Florence had mixed reactions to the camp, but the nation was at war and it was the duty of the city to be accommodating as long as the military was acting reasonably. Housing undesirables wasn't a completely new idea for those living in Florence, since the town was home to a state prison built in 1908 that is still in operation today.[29]

Residents who did oppose the camp made sure their

voices were heard. Members of the Superior Rotary Club thought a POW camp would threaten the local copper mines and railways. There was added anxiety that relatives of German and Italian POWs would move nearby to be close to their loved ones, posing a new layer of threats and uncertainties. Edward Dentzer, vice president of the Magma-Arizona Railroad Company, wrote to Arizona senator Carl Hayden about his displeasure: "I feel sure that a lot of these people would be potential saboteurs and, therefore, a menace to any defense industries in this locality."[30] The U.S. military felt the concerns were unfounded, and the construction of the camp went on as planned.

When Frederick arrived in Florence in 1944, the camp already housed at least 1,500 prisoners of war. Italian POWs were the first to arrive in 1943, and they were quickly put to work picking cotton in the sun-drenched fields. Cotton was still Arizona's most important and lucrative agricultural crop. Defense contractors needed massive amounts to produce military uniforms and other products. In the peak month of November 1943, an average of 1,549 prisoners picked fifty-four pounds of cotton apiece most days, which totaled just shy of two million pounds for the month alone.[31]

Prison populations shifted regularly and the Italians were eventually relocated to another camp. Once Italy surrendered in September 1943, and changed allegiance to the Allied forces, the treatment of the Italian POWs loosened up considerably. The Italian prisoners who were already in captivity couldn't be released, but they were given more freedom and jobs that were off-limits to German POWs. The Italian prisoners at Camp Florence were subsequently moved to labor camps in California in the summer of 1944, as trainloads of German prisoners took their place in the cotton fields in Arizona.[32]

For security concerns, the Americans sought to separate hard-core Nazis from soldiers like Frederick, who never became indoctrinated into Hitler's racist system. But it wasn't an easy task because even in captivity, hard-core Nazis did their best to threaten and maintain control over lower-ranked prisoners, who were more susceptible to American influence. Despite being captured, the German POWs attempted to maintain a hierarchical rule of order within their units. They established a system to settle disputes among themselves and convey issues or requests to their American captors. There was a structure put in place in each camp, where there was one main POW who acted as a liaison between the camp commander and the German POWs. This role typically was given to the highest-ranking prisoner, but on occasion the man who was the most respected and most liked attained the title.[33] Frederick spoke English, which meant he could have been the liaison, but given his personality and distaste for the war from the beginning, it's unlikely that he was a spokesperson in any official capacity.

Like the other prisoners, upon arrival Frederick was processed and received special clothing: a loose-fitting cotton button-down jacket and matching pair of pants with the letters "PW" written in large white block letters across the back of each garment. The uniform was baggy and shapeless, akin to a pair of pajamas but in sturdier fabric, a far cry from the military uniforms the German soldiers had worn before getting caught by the Allies.

The POWs then walked in single file to the prison barracks. The rooms had bunk beds, and a chair and dresser for each prisoner. The accommodations, though sparse, were a surprising relief after the cramped ocean journey and the long train ride. With the exception of the double rows of barbed-wire fences, the conditions in the POW camp looked decent and sanitary, and the POWs were treated with respect. No one had anticipated being greeted with "Good morning" or "Good afternoon," but those pleasantries were commonplace—a fact that surprised the POWs, who knew how inhospitable the Germans could be toward their prisoners.

Perhaps inevitably, there were prisoners who tried to escape from camp. If that ever happened, American guards were trained to shout "Halt" three times before shooting. And if a shooting did occur, assuming it was justified, the guard was to receive a carton of cigarettes and a transfer to another unit.[34] The chances of successfully fleeing Camp Florence were slim, given its location. A former POW there, Paul Zürn, described the futility of trying: "Escape from Camp Florence was impossible. We were behind three rows of barbed wire with guards and guard dogs.

We wore distinct POW clothes, U.S. Army clothes dyed black with 'PW' all over them. The heels of our shoes were notched in such a way that our footprints would be very distinct if we ever did get out. There was a large sign in our compound that said, 'Where will you flee to?' Mexico was over 100 miles away across the hot desert. Escape would have been suicide."[35] Camp Florence's hopeless location notwithstanding, there were numerous reported attempts of prisoner escapes at camps throughout the United States, but they were overwhelmingly unsuccessful. By the end of the war, a total of fifty-six German POWs who tried to escape were shot and killed. A final report by the War Department in November 1947 revealed that out of the 371,000 Germans detained in the United States, 2,222 attempted to escape, and only 17 remained at large.[36]

It was no secret that Germany was losing the war. And the demeanor of the prisoners was constantly observed to see how many of them still maintained allegiance to Hitler. Most of the prisoners at Camp Florence signed a document that had been prepared by POWs at Fort Devens, Massachusetts, in which the German people were advised "to cease hostilities and oust the Nazis." If they signed the honor statement denouncing fascism, they were rewarded with more freedom. The military interrogated POWs to determine which ones weren't a threat to civilians or capable of escaping. Frederick was deemed nonthreatening, as were most POWs at Camp Florence, which was known to have the less fanatical German soldiers in its population.

The uncooperative and unrepentant Nazis at Florence were housed in a separate compound, and many were transferred to Camp Rupert in Paul, Idaho, which had a population of approximately three thousand people.[37] Camp Rupert received the German and Italian POWs with disciplinary problems. The prisoners who attempted sit-down strikes or tried to escape landed there, along with true Nazis who threatened any German POWs who denounced Hitler. Those who were part of the Waffen SS, the brutal security forces associated with the most heinous war crimes, were usually housed at Camp Rupert.[38]

At Florence, in the last year of the war, there were only thirty-eight SS men, who could be identified by the characteristic symbol tattooed under their left arm. In the last year of the war a report to the Office of the Provost Marshal General, the arm of the military that oversaw POWs, indicated that most of the SS officers were so morally beaten down that Nazi fanaticism was largely nonexistent at Camp Florence. "The Nazi influence has been sufficiently diluted to make this camp fertile field for the reorientation program," the report stated, indicating that the Germans were ready to turn on their leader and embrace the teachings of democracy.[39] The POWs who had renounced Hitler would begin to have direct contact with American civilians as a result of their amenable demeanor, working as much as possible.

There was a surprising amount of freedom at Camp Florence once the prisoners had established to the Americans' satisfaction that they weren't spies or fascists. There were religious services held at a stone Catholic chapel that had been built by the Italian prisoners when they first occupied the camp. The chapel was in constant use and attendance steadily increased for both Catholic and Protestant services.[40]

There was even a POW paper called *Der Ruf.* Captain Weiskircher, a high-ranking POW at Camp Florence, recommended that a camp newspaper be established, and an Austrian prisoner with previous newspaper experience acted as the editor.[41]

The POW environment was designed to create a community for captured men to be contained and somewhat comfortable, which the government hoped would increase the prisoners' likelihood of allegiance to the United States. In some of the camps, including Florence, the POWs had it better than their loved ones back home in Germany. There was a PW canteen, where prisoners could buy soap, toothpaste, shaving materials, and of course cigarettes with the money they earned from working, in the form of coupons. Some of the prisoners who worked as waiters in the mess hall would receive fifty-cent or one-dollar tips from the wives of the American officers who liked them and thought they were "good boys."[42] And Florence wasn't the exception. Prisoners at other camps were treated well too. POW Fritz Haus couldn't believe how plentiful the food was. "We lacked nothing. If anything they pampered us. Food was sufficient, regular, and much better than what our German civilians and military had available back home."[43]

Not all of the prisoners were treated well. Some of the conditions for POWs who had to pick cotton were reported as deplorable. Karl-Heinz Hackbarth, who was at a camp in Michigan, remembered seeing a bunch of German POW transfers arrive looking deathly skinny. They had been detained in Texas and Mississippi, where they picked cotton all day in the blazing sun, supposedly without water and never receiving enough food to eat. "They looked like skeletons. We were able to give them some of our food. Of course a lot of American POWs held in Germany also lost fifty or more pounds. So I never saw this mistreatment as something terribly one-sided."[44]

With POWs and American civilians living in such close proximity on a regular basis, fraternization was inevitable, even though it was forbidden. Many residents had an uncontrollable desire to observe the POWs and to communicate with them. They were impressed by the prisoners' youthfulness, physical fitness, and adherence to discipline. In some instances, they responded to them as if they were American farm boys. "Whatever poisonous ideologies may still be boiling underneath their sun-bleached hair to all outward appearances they are like any American kids from Tampa to Tacoma," said one reporter about POWs in Oklahoma.[45]

With Frederick's low rank in the military, he had to take on whatever work the United States Army wanted him to do. With a combination of luck and English fluency, he landed a job mostly working as a cook for the officers' mess.

Most people didn't want to rise before dawn, but POWs like Frederick worked in the kitchen as much as possible. Being there kept them from hard labor in the fields, and allowed them their sparse wages under the terms of the Geneva Convention.

Just like in any military setting, routines and schedules were strictly set for the POWs, and their days started early. Cooks gathered in the mess hall at 4:00 a.m. to begin assembling the morning meals. Breakfast was served directly after 6:00 a.m. roll call. Everyone was fed well; breakfasts consisted of cereal and fruit followed by pancakes, sausage, and bacon. There was one unpopular meal that caused a stream of complaints: a mixture of dried beef and cream sauce on toast, which was known at the camp as SOS, short for "shit on a shingle."[46]

No one would ever say anything negative about Frederick's cooking. He was an excellent baker, specializing in breads and pastries. His mother, Margarete, was a wonderful cook and he had inherited her skills in the kitchen. While he worked, he wore an apron, white cap, white shirt, and khaki pants. He made *brötchen* and *weizenbrote*, some of the German breads he had grown up eating, from scratch. In the kitchen he could forget that he was a prisoner of war. He didn't have to wear his bulky "PW" ensemble either. The guards loosened the reins considerably and Frederick wore regular clothes purchased on base at the supply store.

He would have lived in the kitchen if he could have—anything to avoid picking cotton. Many POWs made sure to prove themselves essential to the goings-on during meal prep and milked it for all they could, particularly during the holidays. They volunteered to prepare Christmas dinner, to help celebrate the occasion and create a sense of community among themselves and the guards. They prepared heaping servings of turkey, potatoes, creamed peas, pumpkin pie, and coffee. And at Christmas the head prisoner on kitchen duty handed each guard a pack of cigarettes as a gift.[47]

Yet the holiday cheer didn't extend to everyone at Camp Florence. For black nurses, there was little to celebrate. For them, and for all African Americans in uniform, the cordial treatment of German POWs from the U.S. military stirred up profound resentment. Or, as was the case with Elinor, feelings of deep disgust.

Gladys Farrow Powell   *William Lawrence Powell*

Margarete Albert   *Karl Albert*

The parents, circa the Great War, 1918

Little Elinor holding a doll in Milton, Massachusetts, circa 1924

Charlotte and baby Frederick in Oppeln, Germany, circa 1925

Charlotte and Frederick, circa 1930

Outside in the garden in Oppeln: Karl, Charlotte,
baby Frederick and Margarete, circa 1925–1926

Karl, Margarete, little Frederick, and
Charlotte at home, circa 1927

Elinor in Milton, Massachusetts, circa 1932

*Elinor's childhood house
on Emerson Road in
Milton, Massachusetts*

*William and Ella
Powell's house on
Granite Place
in Milton*

Charlotte, Margarete, and Frederick at home in Vienna for Christmas, circa 1939

Frederick with his father, Karl Albert

Frederick, circa 1942

Elinor, circa 1942

Elinor with her fellow classmates at the Lincoln School for Nurses in the Bronx, New York, circa 1941–1943

Frederick and fellow Wehrmacht soldiers, circa 1943–1944

Elinor enlists in the U.S. Army Nurse Corps in Fort Huachuca, Arizona, July 1944

Elinor with a fellow army nurse at POW Camp Florence, circa 1944–1945

Elinor outside the barracks

*Frederick wearing his chef's hat along with other POWs
assigned to the mess hall*

*German prisoners of war at Camp Florence, Arizona,
circa 1944–1946*

Elinor, a few months after Stephen's birth in Milton, Massachusetts, spring 1947

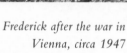

Frederick after the war in Vienna, circa 1947

Elinor and Frederick together again, Milton, summer 1947

Frederick, Elinor, and Stephen set sail for a new life in Germany, July 1952

Frederick, Chris, Elinor, and Stephen in Media, Pennsylvania, circa 1955

Frederick in the woods outside the family home in Fairfield County, Connecticut, circa 1957

Frederick and Chris, circa 1957

Frederick and Elinor in Village Creek, South Norwalk, Connecticut, circa 1960s

5.

Prisoners and Nurses

Feeling lonely and isolated was something that black nurses and prisoners of war had in common in Florence. The POWs were confined to certain areas for security reasons, but the nurses' restrictions were imposed because of the color of their skin.

Florence, like Fort Huachuca, wasn't located near any major cities in Arizona. Both Phoenix and Tucson were more than an hour's drive away. The same isolation that the black nurses felt in basic training was now magnified with the presence of Nazi soldiers and the absence of black men. To make matters worse, there was not an officers' club for blacks at Camp Florence, as there had been at Fort Huachuca. For black nurses, enduring POW Camp Florence meant accepting complete segregation, socially and institutionally.

Depending on the location, both American GIs and POWs could be treated in the same hospital wards. Of course, that didn't always work out so well. German POWs were attacked occasionally, as was the case at Fort Custer in Michigan. "There were wounded American soldiers in the camp hospital, and one of them hit a prisoner with his crutch and another drove his wheelchair into several of the POWs. It was a reaction and I could understand it. We were healthy looking, and these American boys were all shot up," said Karl-Heinz Hackbarth."[1]

Elinor was miserable. There were rarely any emergency surgeries at the Florence hospital, and the nurses had a great deal of free time on their hands, but Jim Crow limited their options.

Gwyneth Blessitt Moore and Elinor became friends at Camp Florence in 1944. Moore remembered how frustrated Elinor would become because of segregation. "We'd head to town and would have to turn right back around to base because no one would serve us," Moore said. "One time some of the white physicians from New York accompanied us and were so horrified that Elinor and I couldn't get served. They returned right back to base with us but they were embarrassed, and kept apologizing."[2] Elinor and Gwyneth appreciated the solidarity of some of the white doctors who were appalled by the discrimination, but it didn't erase their feelings of humiliation. Some restaurants offered them the option of ordering their food in the back of the restaurant near the rear door, as if that were a reasonable alternative rather than another racist slight. Of course the ladies declined the offer.

In some cases when word got back to the commanding

officer about restaurants refusing to serve blacks in uniform, all base personnel would be told not to frequent the establishment again. But that type of response largely depended on the beliefs of the commander in charge and whether he was a segregationist or not. At Camp Rupert in Idaho, one particular commanding officer would let the German POWs walk or loll on the grass, but if a black nurse did, he'd get on his P.A. system and order her off. He also called one African American nurse to his office who reportedly overheard him tell his secretary, "That's one of those smart niggers. When I see these black she-apes in officers' uniforms it makes me so mad I could puke."[3]

Gwyneth handled Jim Crow better than Elinor. She was originally from New Orleans and lived there for a portion of her childhood before moving to the Northeast, so she knew exactly how the rules of Jim Crow worked. "Whites Only" signs didn't send Gwyneth into a rage, and when locals in Phoenix or around Camp Florence were nasty to her, she looked the other way because she'd learned how to brush those slights off as a child.

German POWs were treated better in every aspect of their lives than a great many black Americans, and especially in terms of the freedom and respect they enjoyed when they worked outside of camp and went inside white establishments, including striking up conversations with local residents or attendants at gas stations and train depots. It was also not uncommon for prisoners who were contracted out to work at outside farms to develop friendships with farmers and their children.[4] The differential treatment given to German prisoners and black Americans did not go unnoticed by the POWs, despite the U.S. government's attempt to avoid addressing the glaring hypocrisy. The military wouldn't dare have reading material in the POW camp library that portrayed America in a negative light, including anything about race relations between blacks and whites under Jim Crow, so German POWs did not see the regular commentary about discrimination toward black soldiers and nurses in the *Pittsburgh Courier*, the *Chicago Defender*, *Ebony*, or newsletters from the NAACP, but they witnessed it. And when POWs did confront white American officers about the conditions for blacks, they were told that discrimination was a result of slavery but tremendous progress was being made.[5]

The prisoners learned the limitations of such racial "progress" as they worked alongside black civilians in the cotton fields and in service industries. A surprising camaraderie developed as African Americans began to share their experiences of second-class citizenship at the hands of their own government.[6]

Some POWs who resented picking cotton and considered it low-level and demeaning work commented on how blacks were treated. Corporal Hein Severloh, a German POW at Camp McCain, in Mississippi, said, "We picked cotton the length of the Mississippi. I'm an agriculturalist and I know how to handle hard work, but there it was truly very, very hard. It was terribly hot, and we had to bend over all day. We had nothing to drink. . . . There were a great number of Blacks on the plantation. They required us to gather 100 pounds of cotton a day; but of the blacks they demanded two or three times more. . . . For them it was worse than for us. And you have to see how they lived. Their farms: very ugly, very primitive. These people were so exploited."[7]

It was impossible for African Americans not to compare their experiences with those of German prisoners of war. One black soldier noted that there was a segregated bathroom for blacks at a POW camp in Texas, but German prisoners used the same bathroom as white Americans. Germans fighting for Hitler could use facilities reserved for whites, but black Americans, including those serving in the military to defeat Hitler and preserve democracy, were relegated to segregated latrines. One black soldier wrote, "Seeing this was honestly disheartening. It made me feel, here, the tyrant is placed over the liberator."[8]

In April 1944, in El Paso, Texas, nine black soldiers were denied access to the train station's main dining room. Standing there in uniform, they could not get service. But about two dozen German POWs with their guards entered the same dining room and were immediately seated without objection. "They entered the lunchroom, sat at the tables, had their meals served, talked, smoked, in fact had quite a swell time," wrote a black soldier, who along with the other African Americans was forced to sit in the waiting area, hungry and humiliated. He asked, "Why are they treated better than we are?" The letter, which was sent to the army weekly, *Yank*, was reprinted in multiple outlets and created an outcry of protest, but not enough to end segregation in the armed services.[9]

Roy Wilkins, then the editor of *The Crisis*, the official magazine of the NAACP, said, "Nothing so lowers Negro morale as the frequent preferential treatment of Axis prisoners of war in contrast with deprecatory treatment of Army policy towards American troops who happen to be Negro."[10]

The reality, however painful, was that segregation in the military was considered acceptable behavior throughout the United States. A 1942 survey of white soldiers from the North and South revealed that the majority of them shared similar attitudes about segregation in the army regardless of region. White enlisted men from the North showed a strong prejudice against sharing recreational facilities with Negro troops; white soldiers from border states showed an even stronger dislike; and whites from the South showed the strongest prejudice of all. There were a few marked differences depending on education level—the more educated people were, the more liberal they tended to be in their attitude about segregation. But overall, very few objected to the segregated status of blacks.[11]

Elinor and Gwyneth bided their time, uninterested and listless. Fortunately, there were horses at Camp Florence, and the two women would ride trails together at sunset. But they were mostly confined to the hospital, trying to keep themselves busy. The POWs were generally in good physical health, but an appendectomy or other surgery was necessary from time to time. And some prisoners came down with common colds and viruses that required checkups and bedside nursing. At times a new crop of prisoners from Europe or North Africa arrived with malaria and would have to be sequestered. There was a 7:30 a.m. "sick call" every day, which entailed a march to the hospital for anyone seeking medical treatment, and there were routine physical examinations performed every two months, primarily to check for scabies, hernias, and venereal disease.[12]

Still, the thirty to forty black nurses who were stationed at Florence were largely underutilized. They also had no social outlets to cope with the loneliness of military life. If trying to find establishments that served them was challenging, dating was almost impossible. There were no black soldiers at Camp Florence. "There wasn't a Negro man within a hundred miles of that camp. Everyone was white, except for us," said Ora Hicks, a black nurse stationed there.[13]

The nurses' interactions with the opposite sex came in the form of friendly conversations with a few of the doctors from the North. But even those innocent encounters could backfire, as Dorothy Jenkins learned.

Jenkins was around the same age as Elinor when she joined the U.S. Army Nurse Corps. Born and raised in Oklahoma, she attended nursing school at Prairie View A&M University, a historically black college in Texas, because there weren't any nursing schools in Oklahoma that admitted black women at the time.

After she completed her nursing degree, Jenkins joined the Red Cross at the encouragement of her nursing instructors. Like Elinor, she became energized by the idea of serving her country in World War II. Army nurses were also paid much better than civilian nurses, a fact that black women could not overlook considering how much less they were paid than their white counterparts.

The Naval Nurse Corps rejected Jenkins. "I remember the letter," she said. "It said, 'We regret to inform you that we are not accepting Negro nurses at this time.' " Consequently, Jenkins applied to the Army Nurse Corps while working at a hospital in New York City, and upon acceptance was sent to Camp McCoy, Wisconsin, for basic training in October of 1944.

Jenkins breezed through the six weeks of drills and exercises, all supervised by white nurses. "It was beautiful there and the supervising nurses were all very nice. But I remember that they weren't experienced in segregation," she said. "They sent a photo of us in uniform to our hometown newspapers. They sent mine to the *Daily Oklahoman*, who returned it and told them to find a black paper."

Although that experience was embarrassing, Jenkins had grown up in a segregated state and had already developed a thick skin. But things quickly soured when she completed basic training and left for Fort Huachuca. After a few weeks there, she was sent to Camp San Luis Obispo in California to care for Italian and Japanese POWs.

"I was surprised to have been sent to a prisoner of war

camp," she said. "Due to the integrated experience in New York, it was disappointing to go to POW camps, which segregated us."

Jenkins tried to make the best of her experience at the camp, but she soon learned that she would never be happy as a black nurse in the army. She befriended a Jewish warrant officer from New York, who invited her to the officers' club with him one evening. When they walked in together, a silence filled the room, and everyone stared at Jenkins and the officer, giving them nasty looks and purposely bumping them while passing by. "They would walk close to us and give us an evil eye. We were told to leave and never to come back. Apparently, my presence upset the white officers and their wives, even though I was an officer in the army too." Her friend was shipped overseas shortly after the episode, and Jenkins was transferred to Camp Papago Park, a German POW camp in Arizona. "It definitely was punishment," she said.[14]

Camp Papago Park was closer to Phoenix, but that didn't change the isolating experience for black nurses like Jenkins, who found themselves routinely left out of army meetings and official social functions hosted by the white officers stationed there. At times the discrimination was so pervasive that some white officers would reprimand and insult black nurses in front of the German prisoners or, worse, allow the POWs to be disrespectful as well.

In the hospital ward, one German POW told an African American nurse that he hated "niggers." The nurse reported the incident to the commanding officer of Camp Papago Park with an assumption that the German POW would be sent back to his barracks and punished. But later that day she found out that nothing had happened to him. The nurse wrote to Mabel Staupers detailing the injustice. The German POW was able to plead his case to Colonel Moore, a Texan described in the letter as "the officer who refused to shake hands with the new Negro doctors when Huachuca was first opened." Once Moore heard the POW's side of things, the prisoner was allowed to stay put without a reprimand. "That is the worst insult an army officer should ever have to take," wrote the nurse. "I think it is insult enough to be out here taking care of them when we volunteered to come into the army to nurse military personnel. . . . It is sickening to see the treatment given to these prisoners when our own men are actually suffering from lack of food and good treatment. All of this is making us very bitter." [15]

Whoever was in charge of a given camp would set the tone for racial tolerance. If the most powerful person was a staunch segregationist, then the environment for African Americans would be oppressive. At Camp Florence, there had been commanding officers who allowed black nurses to eat in the same dining area as white officers, and there were other COs who did not want blacks and whites eating together at all, which was the way it was when Elinor arrived. But no matter how many letters Mabel Staupers received from nurses pleading for relief, the military ignored them.

Oneida Miller Stuart's experience in the army only reinforced how indefensible the conditions remained for many black nurses, even toward the end of the war. Stuart was called "nigger" habitually. A black nurse who entered the U.S. Army Nurse Corps in 1945, Stuart was sent to Nichols Army Hospital in Louisville, Kentucky, where large numbers of wounded Allied men were returning from battle. There, both black and white soldiers were patients, as well as German POWs. Naturally, the black nurses overwhelmingly tended to the African American enlisted men and German prisoners, but depending on demand, they found themselves caring for white American soldiers too. "We were called 'nigger' many a times," said Miller. "But you just kept on going. They'd say, 'Nigger don't you put your hands on me.' It would really get to me sometimes."

On her days off, Stuart would go into Louisville to look at dresses in various retail shops, but she couldn't try anything on. Even as a member of the military, she, as a black woman, was only allowed to hold the piece up to herself in the mirror.[16]

The German POWs at Camp Florence had arguably a better social life than the nurses did. The prisoners had a regular presence in the town of Florence, since they were hired out to work in the cotton fields, in Laundromats, or in plants. That put the POWs in close contact with local women daily. They were told not to go near any women, but fraternization was a fairly common occurrence.[17]

Ray Radeke, a guard at Camp Florence, was always

perplexed by the attention the local residents showered on the POWs. They were fascinated by them and always wanted to sneak glimpses. He noticed how young women would linger around areas where German POWs were working in Phoenix, and on more remote job sites Radeke saw women intentionally position themselves on an elevated area to sunbathe where the prisoners could see them.

The guards were also aware of the potential for relationships between POWs and nonwhite women. Hans Lammersdorf, a POW at Camp Papago Park, was shocked when a white guard told him to stay away from black and Mexican women because they were inferior. "These Americans, they were officers, told us to be ashamed of mixing with those people," he said. The words were almost identical to the warnings the Germans had given Lammersdorf about mixing with Polish people. "So here in America they were telling us the same thing, basically."[18]

Lammersdorf and many other POWs were shocked by the racism in the United States and how prejudice was accepted and preached as openly as it was in Germany, and it wasn't just a lone deranged guard spouting white supremacist ideology. Lammersdorf, while en route to a POW camp in Arizona, discovered that discrimination toward blacks was systemic and institutional. "On the train from Houston . . . to Papago Park, they had separated the Whites and the Blacks. We prisoners of war were in the White compartments. We were not with the Blacks. They had their own compartments. In the railroad station in Houston we saw the separated facilities. The restrooms, Black and White. We looked at it and thought 'By golly, what's going on here?' " Once in Arizona, a few guards pulled Lammersdorf and the other prisoners aside and talked to them about racial purity. "We were amused that Americans could criticize us for racial prejudice when they had some of their own." [19]

But not all American citizens were intrigued by German POWs. By the last year of the war, Phoenix residents were getting fed up with what they perceived as careless supervision of the German POWs. In particular, residents of Chandler, a suburb near Phoenix, were offended by the prisoners "riding through the middle of town, ogling the girls and whistling at and insulting them." [20]

The presence of POWs was a sore point for many of Chandler's residents. The prisoners were transported almost daily through town, and their freedom took locals by surprise. On one occasion, a soldier-guard reportedly had been drinking and allowed a Nazi prisoner to carry his rifle as they strolled down the road. The guard was placed on thirty-day suspension. [21] The monotonous routine of a POW camp contributed to a comfort level between the prisoners and the American guards at Camp Florence, and a loosening of protocol. The prisoners and guards were in the same age-group, usually late teens to mid-20s, and there also was a mutual understanding of what serving in the military meant. Eventually the conditions became so lax that in an inspection report the camp was cited for lack of discipline.

The "prisoners at base camp and branch camps were seen working in shorts and without any upper garments both in camp and on private contract work," it stated.[22]

If the guards at Camp Florence preached racial superiority to Frederick, or if their friendships with other prisoners crossed boundaries, it had little impact on him. He had carved out a peaceful existence for himself that didn't include fascist ideology or racial prejudice. Cooking and listening to music were his sustenance.

Jazz played a big role in Frederick's ability to cope with the monotony that came with being a prisoner of war. He had the sounds of New Orleans at his fingertips, which provided comfort and healing from the pain of his childhood. He felt intimately connected to jazz and the black musicians who performed it, even though Frederick's interactions with blacks were largely nonexistent. He didn't know any people of color in Oppeln, nor when his family later moved to Vienna. He envisioned black people as warm, passionate, and artistic, but that was based on a fantasy he'd spun and not on experiences he'd had. He was only nineteen years old when he was captured—daydreaming was part of his existence, along with raging hormones, and listening to music seemed to calm his restlessness.

With regular access to U.S. Armed Forces Radio, he followed several black musicians, such as Billie Holiday, Duke Ellington, Count Basie, and Ella Fitzgerald.[23] And if there was a record player around, he could play one of the guards'

V-Discs, which were special phonograph records produced just for U.S. military personnel. The V-Discs played an active role in the lives of Americans stationed all over the world. They were the product of a special arrangement between the United States Army and private recording companies from 1943 to 1949. Many popular bands and singers, from Louis Armstrong to Frank Sinatra to Bing Crosby, recorded for the V-Disc program. Some of the discs also contained introductions by bandleaders and artists, wishing the soldiers good luck and offering prayers.[24]

The propaganda meant nothing to Frederick because he had always had only one opinion of the war—that it was wrong. For him, music represented the warmth he never received as a child. There was nothing he could look back on in his upbringing that made him nostalgic about his relationship with his father. He didn't have memories of Karl teaching him how to fish, camp, or talk to girls, because none of that ever happened. And he also didn't know what real committed love looked like, because his parents didn't have a loving marriage. With his father away every weekend with his girlfriend, Frederick knew only infidelity, loneliness, and betrayal. He had no idea what true romantic love felt like, but when he listened to jazz he longed for it.[25]

The dysfunction of Margarete and Karl's relationship fueled Frederick's desire to have a genuine relationship with a woman. He didn't want any arrangement or obligation for the sake of keeping up appearances. He wanted an intense bond with a woman who would be by his side and make him feel valued as a man. And he associated his passion for love with music by African Americans.

It seemed like a typical late summer afternoon. It was scorching hot outside as usual, and Frederick was relieved that his kitchen duties allowed him to wear lightweight clothing. He normally didn't venture out into the mess hall, as every POW had his designated role. The cooks stayed in the kitchen; the servers worked the main floor. But every now and then, those in the back wanted to see what was happening out front. And that day, Frederick glimpsed into the dining area. Not long before, a group of black nurses had been transitioned into the hospital staff. Since most of the POWs had never spent any time around black people, the nurses' arrival did not go unnoticed.

A profound feeling overcame Frederick when he spotted a beautiful, tall black woman. He had never felt so drawn to a complete stranger before. It was if he had been hypnotized when he first made eye contact with Elinor. She walked in with other nurses and headed toward their designated eating area, which was removed from the tables where white officers and physicians sat. Frederick didn't see anyone else in the room. She was striking at six feet tall, and her impeccable posture gave her a regal quality; her mother had always told her daughters to stand up straight the way dignified and important women did.

Incapable of concentrating on his kitchen duties, Frederick bypassed the POW waiters and walked right up to

Elinor. He looked her in the eyes, smiled, and said with a German accent, "You should know my name. I'm the man who is going to marry you."[26]

Flattered and relatively shocked, Elinor smiled. She later giggled with Gwyneth about the encounter. Who was this POW approaching her in the mess hall so boldly? Flirting with a German prisoner of war was the furthest thing from Elinor's mind. He was probably just a kid, anyway. She remembered being told that some of the POWs were as young as fifteen.[27] In 1944, Elinor was twenty-three years old. If she had been anywhere else—Boston, New York, or even Fort Huachuca—she would have had the attention of numerous African American men, but that was not going to happen in Florence. She had to admit that the handsome German made her day a bit lighter.

It wasn't a complete shock to Elinor that a white man found her attractive. She had true friendships with white people growing up in Massachusetts, as did her parents. But it's not entirely clear if Elinor had ever shared a romance with a man of a different race.

Still, she figured the encounter with Frederick was amusing and harmless, a onetime episode. POWs were bored, as bored as the nurses. She had just met one who wanted to have some fun. A simple flirtation, nothing else.

Frederick had trouble sleeping after he met Elinor. He couldn't stop thinking about her. He didn't even get her first name because he had to rush back to the kitchen. He only saw that her badge said "Powell." He would volunteer to serve as many meals as possible so he could see her, stare at her, and get to know her. He hadn't felt joyous or passionate about something for a long time. Now suddenly he felt alive, and he knew he had fallen in love. It sounded ridiculous and immature, and given his background, the fact that she was black also made it incomprehensible. But Frederick knew something magical had happened when he looked into Elinor's eyes. She was what he had been waiting for all his life.[28]

6.

A Forbidden Romance

FREDERICK HAD FALLEN IN LOVE AT FIRST SIGHT. He had limited experience with women, but his desire for Elinor was genuine, raw, and unburdened by any remnants of Nazi doctrine. His life had changed instantaneously the moment he spotted her in the officers' mess. Everything about his POW experience shifted from dull and routine to thrilling and purposeful. Elinor became the key to his happiness; she was the focus of all his thoughts. And Frederick was determined to do everything in his power to ensure the feelings were reciprocated.

He wanted to pursue an intimate and exclusive relationship. But with no power, money, or freedom—and an extremely regimented POW existence—this seemed very unlikely. Despite their relaxed disposition, his American captors still dictated everything about his daily life. He showered when he was told to shower. He ate when he was told to eat. He worked when he was told to work, getting up at when the sky was still black to bake bread and prepare the meals for the day. But the one thing he had control over were his dreams and desires, and that was enough encouragement for him to get through the other tasks. He was not going to let his prisoner status infringe on his strategy to pursue Elinor.

Several POWs figured out ways to rendezvous with local women, but those were mostly physical encounters. Elinor awakened a longing in Frederick that was beyond carnal. Naturally, the physical attraction was strong. She was tall, curvaceous, and stunning. But there was an emotional connection he felt immediately that needed to be explored as well. He later said it was as though he had been put under a spell from the first time he laid eyes on her.[1]

Frederick's calculated plan came down to seeing Elinor every day at mealtime. And if it couldn't be every day, then it would be every other day. Even if for a moment, he wanted to lock eyes with her and subliminally tell her that he wanted her and that she was the most exotic woman he had ever met. And it wasn't in a fetishizing way; he truly was enamored and intrigued.

It wasn't long before Elinor began to enjoy and look forward to Frederick's playful antics. When he peeked out of the kitchen to tip his chef's hat in her direction and gaze into her eyes, even if briefly, the attention satisfied a need in her that she had suppressed as an army nurse. She hadn't felt excitement since setting foot in Florence, and she couldn't deny that a marriage proposal at a first meeting was a big boost to her ego, which had taken quite a beating since her enlistment. The segregated military made for a very lonely social life. Yet it hadn't occurred to Elinor to ever look at a German prisoner in a romantic way: they were captured soldiers, enemies of war, and Nazis. Hitler's views about nonwhites were well known. How could an African American think about intimacy with a German?

But there was something different about Frederick. His mannerisms, warmth, and obvious attraction to her all softened her guarded exterior. And Frederick was handsome, tall, and lean, with chiseled features. Elinor was twenty-three years old, after all, an age where a glorious-looking man, regardless of race or ethnicity, made her giddy and curious. She also felt a sense of justice at being desired by a German soldier, a member of the very group the U.S. military thought wouldn't be interested in her, or any black nurse for that matter, hence their regular assignments at POW camps.

Frederick's attraction demonstrated complete disregard for Jim Crow. And Elinor needed to see someone stand up against it. If kindness came from a soldier in Hitler's army, Elinor decided, then she would welcome it. She would soon discover that a number of German prisoners were not the fascist bigots she had anticipated and, in fact, were friendlier to her than some of the local white people in Arizona, who were her fellow American citizens.

Gwyneth, as one of Elinor's closest friends at Camp Florence, was also pleasantly surprised by the kindness of some of the German POWs. "They were always very nice to us, really," she said. "I was never taught to hate anybody, and

I didn't even feel hate towards the Germans for the entire war or anything like that." One of the prisoners made a wooden nameplate for her with "Gwyneth" etched into the surface—an endearing memento that she saved.[2]

Ora Hicks, during her time at Camp Florence, felt the POWs were grateful to receive her care. "They never called us names or nothing like that," she said. Hicks thought many of the German prisoners were homesick and found comfort in talking to the nurses about themselves, their families, and their girlfriends. "When your life is at stake, you better be nice because we might be the one to save your life."[3] Ironically, the discrimination that many black nurses experienced came from white American officers, not POWs. Complaints of racism from black nurses were documented in several states across the country, but most happened in the Deep South and Southwest, where black nurses tended to be stationed.

"I was not naive regarding segregation and discrimination but going into a completely segregated situation was constantly a shock to me," said Elinor years later. "I think I stayed angry most of my army career, even though the whole experience was interesting, maddening, frustrating and even fun."[4]

Gwyneth observed how Elinor could never fully accept segregation during their time at Camp Florence. Unlike Elinor, it didn't bother her as much due to her familiarity with Jim Crow as a child. She never thought of complaining or resisting. "We didn't feel that we should be protesting.

It was if you do well, never get in trouble, and do the right thing that everything's going to be all right. I never felt put down. But I knew and I was aware we were second-class people, but that's the way it was."[5]

It would never be that way for Elinor, however.

Frederick's desire for her flew in the face of society's belief, both German and American, that she was inferior. He could have subscribed to many Americans' sense of white racial superiority, and to the hypocrisies, political and moral, that blacks had to live with. But Frederick made his own beliefs clear: he wanted her, unequivocally. It wasn't long before she encouraged him in his pursuit.

Once their attraction for each other was openly established, Elinor and Frederick were discreet with their flirtation and showed their feelings to each other in harmless ways: frequent smiles in the officers' mess, lingering stares, even a wink or a blown kiss for laughs. As their feelings intensified, they did their best to hide it. Elinor was an officer, and even though she had lost a great deal of respect for the military, she didn't want to ruin her reputation and suffer draconian consequences for frolicking with a POW.

Frederick went to enormous efforts to make Elinor elaborate meals. If meatloaf were on the menu, he would prepare peas and gravy, mashed potatoes, and wiener schnitzel just for her. He also made her apple strudel. Elinor loved every minute of it.

None of the guards were suspicious. They rarely interacted with the black nurses, and the last thing they would have anticipated was a romance unfolding right in front of them between a German POW and a black officer.

Soon the brief flirtations and sightings of Elinor weren't enough for Frederick. The deeper his desire became, the more creative he had to be in order to spend real time getting to know her. Like at other POW camps in the United States, recreational activities were permitted for the prisoners. Some formed orchestras and put on concerts; others played soccer. Frederick taught baking classes occasionally for anyone who wanted to attend or observe. It turned out to be a brilliant move, as he chose an activity that would appeal to the nurses.

Elinor immediately signed up for a class on a day she wasn't expected to report at the hospital. The nurses were supposed to take turns going to the class so the kitchen wouldn't be overcrowded during the demonstration, but Elinor attended every one without fail. Besides staring at Frederick and listening to his accent, which she loved even though some of the words sounded abrupt and even harsh, the classes gave her something fun to do besides nursing. Her free time until then had been spent on two activities: occasionally riding horses with Gwyneth and playing cards with the other nurses. Now she could add learning to bake German pastries to her short list of positive experiences as an army nurse.[6]

Frederick's class became a hit. As the nurses hovered over a prep table in the kitchen, Frederick showed them how to make *bauernbrot*, with its signature hard crust; *roggenmischbrot*, a sourdough bread made with rye and wheat flour;

and *brötchen* (German rolls) and buns. Elinor did her best to concentrate on the bread rather than daydreaming about Frederick, but her heart pounded as she watched him in his white hat, T-shirt, and apron. During his demos, when he asked a question to be sure everyone was following, Elinor nodded in agreement, barely able to focus. She was falling in love—with a German.

Before long, the baking classes, like his moments with Elinor in the officers' mess, weren't enough; plus there were only so many recipes he could demonstrate with the limited number of ingredients he had at his disposal. He needed to put a much bigger plan into motion, and once he began to volunteer at the hospital, that is what he did. According to his POW card, and despite what his family thought, Frederick had been a low-ranking medic in the Luftwaffe, and he could speak English, which was enough to be considered useful to the medical staff, who always needed translators when treating German POWs. It was an ideal situation. The nurses were never very busy, and Frederick would have plenty of time to spend with Elinor.

The nurses were on duty from 7:00 a.m. to 7:00 p.m., a twelve-hour shift with a few breaks throughout. There weren't many emergencies, so Elinor's schedule was usually free of intense lifesaving activity and critical demands. This meant that she and Frederick were able to find plenty of time to sneak away and be together with little risk of being missed, let alone caught. There weren't many guards roaming the corridors, as the threat of POWs escaping from the hospital was quite low. Only the perimeter of the camp, especially near the POW barracks, was guarded constantly.

The hospital was the ideal place for privacy. The surgery rooms were rarely occupied, and Elinor didn't worry about the other nurses on duty figuring out what was going on. Gwyneth and some of the other women knew something was developing between Elinor and Frederick, but they would have never reported the couple. There was a real sisterhood between the black nurses, who relied on one another a great deal. Elinor also made sure there were plenty of other nurses on hand when she decided to disappear for an hour or so to be with Frederick. On slow days, when there wasn't surgery scheduled, or if a doctor was on an extended lunch break, Elinor slipped away without hesitation.

Every time she met Frederick she was actively defying the military and Jim Crow, a rebellion that gave her delicious satisfaction. She had been told directly that black nurses were stationed at Camp Florence because the army was uncomfortable with fraternization between white nurses and the German POWs. She correctly concluded that the military didn't think black nurses were desirable enough to be compromised in the same way. It was a stinging slight among a host of insults. The military made it clear time and time again that African American army nurses were dispensable. Elinor had finally had enough.

Acting on her feelings toward Frederick allowed her to assert some sense of authority over her life again. The army uniform and the restrictions that came with wearing one became much less important to Elinor. With every touch, Frederick helped to quell the feelings of rejection that she had internalized ever since she joined the U.S. Army Nurse Corps. He was her oasis, and she was willing to put her military career on the line to be with him.[7]

It began with passionate kisses and lingering embraces. If they passed each other in the hallways, they would touch briefly, a light brush on the hands or an accidental collision—anything to feel close to each other. Their coupling took on a symbolic rebellion that made the sexual tension all the more strong. Frederick had dreamed about touching every inch of Elinor from the moment he saw her in the dining room. And finally, after playful flirtations, gazes, and kisses that never lasted long enough, after thinking about her from the moment he got up in the morning until he went to bed at night, and after strategically planning his work schedule to see her as much as possible in the mess hall and in the hospital, Frederick made love to Elinor on an operating table in a surgery room at the Camp Florence hospital.[8]

Their relationship was so scandalous, so risky and so disruptive, that it made Elinor's heart flutter with excitement. After she began sleeping with Frederick, she didn't return to the nurses' barracks and share the intimate details with her friends. She was discreet (despite her obvious euphoria), but soon Elinor began to see Frederick at all hours of the night, which was a clear giveaway that something serious had developed. Gwyneth picked up on it immediately.

The nurses' barracks at Camp Florence had individual private rooms—a requirement for all officers in the army, even black ones, who typically didn't get the same consideration as their white contemporaries. The arrangement was ideal for Elinor because she could avoid waking up a roommate as she slipped in and out of bed to meet Frederick. There were no guards positioned outside the nurses' barracks either. Elinor did need a lookout from time to time, just in case some personnel were lingering around the grounds nearby and might spot her returning at suspicious hours. In such instances, she could always use the excuse of working late at the hospital because of a medical emergency. Gwyneth helped sneak her out on these occasions, and it was obvious to her what was happening. "I could tell she was falling in love. She was private, but the way she looked—we all knew."

Elinor's trysts with Frederick were potentially dangerous. She was in the United States Army Nurse Corps. Her country was at war with the Nazis. A love affair with a German prisoner could have been considered treasonous and the ramifications severe: court-martial, dishonorable discharge, imprisonment. Frederick could have been punished too. But they were blinded to any danger by their love.[9]

Months passed as Elinor and Frederick's flirtations escalated into a full-blown sexual relationship that bonded them emotionally and physically. The two behaved as if they were invincible, as if no one would ever find out. Until, of course, the truth was exposed.

7.

End of War

AFTER FREDERICK AND ELINOR BEGAN SLEEPING together the days of rational thinking disintegrated. Every minute of their existence rested on being together. Frederick split his time volunteering in the hospital and working in the kitchen, and somehow his schedule never sounded any alarms. He had established himself as a trusted hospital volunteer in addition to being a much relied-upon and valued cook in the officers' mess. The guards weren't suspicious of him at all.

Whether he was translating or working as an orderly mopping floors and cleaning rooms, Frederick familiarized himself with every inch of the hospital to find safe places to be alone with Elinor. She helped plot their escapades as well, since she had access to the staff's schedules, which meant she knew exactly when the surgery rooms would be vacant. After the war, in a rare admission, Frederick revealed to his sister, Charlotte, that he and Elinor would make love whenever possible.

The circumstances surrounding Elinor and Frederick's relationship were fitting for a passionate affair. There was absolutely nothing to do in Florence; it was a remote town and they were young, full of sexual desire, and seeking release from their own personal troubles. They were each other's forbidden fruit, and anything that brought them happiness during the war was worth the risk. And the two never seemed to fear getting caught. But Gwyneth was worried for them.

"Since Frederick was in the kitchen as a baker, he was permitted out of his compound at night. So he was over in the areas for the officers doing the cooking and whatnot. And then Elinor would sneak out. I was nervous about the whole situation, but they weren't," Gwyneth said. She admired Elinor for being bold, but began to think she was foolish too. "She knew what could have happened to her," said Gwyneth of the consequences Elinor would have faced had she been caught. She understood, however, the feelings her friend had for Frederick. "They had the greatest love story."

Frederick and Elinor refused to spoil their love affair by worrying about getting exposed. Their youth, coupled with their intense urge for each other, made the risk worth it. And the alternative—to not have each other as lovers and confidants during the war—was unthinkable.

Elinor's initial attraction may have been a subconscious way of telling the U.S. military, Jim Crow, and Nazism to go to hell, but she had since found true love and respect for

Frederick, a German POW who happened to be in Hitler's army by circumstance, not choice. Frederick may have been considered a Nazi by people who automatically associated German soldiers with Nazi ideology, but she knew he wasn't. He didn't harbor feelings of racial superiority. Everything about him was gentle and kind. And Elinor didn't care about the laws she was breaking to be with him.

The idea of loving a woman who was the embodiment of everything he was supposed to loathe excited Frederick. He felt loved and accepted in Elinor's presence, and he subconsciously tied her race to those feelings. She was passionate and warm, exactly the way he imagined African Americans to be in the countless hours he spent listening to the music of black jazz artists. Elinor made him feel like a hero, and her dependence on him gave him the confidence and purpose he had been deprived of while growing up without the approval of his father. And though Frederick knew being intimate with a black woman was a major taboo, he didn't care.

Eventually others began to notice, and at some point rumors began to spread. On one occasion when Frederick was assigned to farm work, to his surprise one of the agricultural captains tried to dissuade him from pursuing Elinor, not because she was an army officer but because she was black.

The arguments and warnings about race mixing had no impact on Frederick whatsoever. He and Elinor continued their after-hours dates. But their luck ran out when one of the guards caught Frederick sneaking around one night.

Whatever made-up excuse he tried to give didn't work, and he was severely beaten by the officers, who also shaved his head as an additional act of humiliation.[1] When prisoners were caught sneaking around where they were not supposed to be their punishment could mean solitary confinement and a diet of water and bread that lasted for days to physically weaken their bodies and fill their heads with paranoid thoughts.[2] Frederick may have endured this along with his beating.

Elinor never got caught, and if the American guards suspected her, they didn't bring her up on charges. She, unlike Frederick, never mentioned receiving a reprimand about her forbidden relationship, nor did Gwyneth ever recall Elinor getting into trouble. In all likelihood Frederick lied to protect her by giving some alternative reason as to why he was roaming around.

Not surprisingly, Frederick's beating wasn't enough to deter him, and he never stopped his romance with Elinor. Their decision to stay together represented a deep sense of courage, passion, and defiance.

Although Elinor had found a lover to soften the edges of her segregated wartime service, black nurses were still very much isolated and bitter about their experience at the POW camp. The U.S. government shamelessly asked more nurses to volunteer for the war effort even while the Army Nurse Corps continued to keep its enlistment numbers of black RNs very low. It was a clear message that the military would rather remain short-staffed than incorporate black nurses into the medical units that treated all Allied soldiers, white and black, regardless of race.

Toward the last year of the war, after D-Day and the bloody Battle of the Bulge, the number of wounded American men reached dangerous levels. With lives at stake, the relegation of black nurses to POW camps while they were needed elsewhere finally began to get the attention of more than just Negro newspapers and Mabel Staupers.

Albert Deutsch, a reporter for *P.M.*, a New York–based daily paper, wrote a damning piece on December 26, 1944, in which he slammed the military for its treatment of eager black nurses. "Nine thousand bewildered and bitter graduate nurses watch with wonder the Army's frantic call for nurses which excludes brown-skinned Angels of Mercy," wrote Deutsch.[3]

On January 4, 1945, an emergency meeting about army nurses took place at the Pierre Hotel in New York City. About three hundred citizens and nurses attended to hear Major General Norman T. Kirk, the U.S. Army surgeon general at the time, make a highly anticipated announcement that a conscription of nurses was under serious consideration given the large number of American soldiers returning home wounded. In the month of December alone, thirty thousand injured Americans came back from war, and he expected another thirty thousand soon after. He calculated that the United States Nurse Corps, which had forty thousand nurses, needed an additional ten thousand nurses immediately, and a draft would be required if volunteer nurses didn't step forward.[4]

Mabel Staupers, who attended the meeting, was outraged by General Kirk's blatant disregard for the talented and willing black nurses who wanted to serve but were passed over. If nurses were in such demand, she asked him, then why did the United States Army Nurse Corps have only three hundred black nurses in its ranks although nine thousand had signed up? And even more volunteers would have stepped forward had word not begun to spread about the poor treatment of black nurses in the army. Kirk responded that the number of black nurses was in proportion to the number of black troops serving in the army, which wasn't true. The fact was black nurses were not called to serve in the same proportion as white nurses. The military was discriminating against black nurses and everyone knew it.[5]

Kirk also reportedly said that the army didn't mix black nurses with white ones. That was another false statement. In 1944 Staupers visited Camp Livingston in Louisiana, where white and black nurses were treating patients of all races because the demand for medical care was so great. The lines of segregation were secondary to the needs of wounded men, as Staupers noted, and there was no reason that practice couldn't be implemented at other military posts throughout the United States.

His erroneous statement makes clear that either General Kirk did not have a grasp on the working lives of black nurses in the U.S. Army Nurse Corps or he didn't know what to do about it or didn't *want* to do anything about it. His dismissive tone confirmed the obvious—no one in the military wanted black nurses to serve or had thoughtfully considered how they were being utilized.

After the meeting, in a joint statement, Staupers and the National Nursing Council for War Service pointed out that General Kirk was wrong about numerous facts: the 330 black nurses in the U.S. Army Nurse Corps accounted for far less than one-tenth the number of Negro soldiers in the army, which was the accepted ratio of nurses to soldiers.

Staupers also addressed another sinister reason the military used to justify the low numbers of black nurses—their qualification. Black and white nurses were required to take the same state board examination, and Staupers provided evidence from the United States Public Health Service that stated, "The standards of the Negro schools do not differ from those of all schools of nursing." She went on to dispel the fallacy that black nurses graduated from schools that did not meet the minimum standards required for all nursing schools. The truth was that more than two-thirds of the thirty schools for black nursing students had a bed capacity of more than fifty, the minimum requirement for military eligibility. About 89 percent of black nurses graduated from schools connected to hospitals that had daily averages of fifty or more patients. Staupers refuted all of the military's excuses for denying black nurses the opportunity to serve in substantial numbers.[6] The real possibility of a nursing draft only reinforced the deliberate shutting out of African American nurses in the war effort.

On January 6, 1945, President Franklin Roosevelt, in his State of the Union Address, called for an amendment to the Selective Service and Training Act that would allow for the conscription of American nurses into the armed forces. With 40,000 nurses in service, FDR called for 18,000 more.

The public's reaction to a possible draft of women was one of shock and confusion, and the finger-pointing came from all directions. A major reason given to explain the nursing shortage was the haphazard recruiting process, which the army had delegated to the American Red Cross since 1942. Others thought the glamorization of the Women's Army Corps, known as the WACs and nicknamed "Those Wonderful G.I. Janes," was more appealing to women because they got to perform all kinds of military jobs compared to nurses. But more troubling were the mixed signals coming from the War Department itself, which in 1943–1944 first raised its enlistment goals for nurses, then lowered them, and then raised them again. There was never a clear-cut number of how many nurses were needed. As a result, misinformation spread quickly. From June to September 1944, the Army Nurse Corps had its lowest numbers of volunteers come forward since the war started. Some attributed this not only to the unclear message about nursing shortages but also to the public belief that the war was almost over.

Representative Andrew J. May of Kentucky, chair of the House Military Affairs Committee, responded to FDR's call with a proposed amendment known as the May Bill. Under his legislation, all unmarried nurses between twenty and forty-five would be eligible for a draft and would enter the army at the rank of private; nurses who volunteered would enter as second lieutenants as incentive for coming forward. The bill also included an anti-discrimination provision to allow black nurses to be eligible as well.[7]

During the period in which the bill was debated, Congressman Adam Clayton Powell Jr., the esteemed African American minister from Harlem, was vocal about discrimination against black nurses by the U.S. military. "It is absolutely unbelievable that in times like these, when the world is going forward, that there are leaders in our American life who are going backward. It is further unbelievable that these leaders have become so blindly and unreasonably un-American that they have forced our wounded men to face the tragedy of death rather than allow trained nurses to aid because these nurses' skins happen to be of a different color."[8] The amendment passed the House almost unanimously. But it stalled in the Senate without any explanation given and was eventually shelved.

The conscription of nurses never occurred—enough of them volunteered to care for the high numbers of wounded men returning from war. But the disregard of black nurses continued.

Undeterred, Mabel Staupers carried on and continued to lobby for an amendment that prohibited the discrimination of black nurses in the military. But the morale of

African American nurses who were currently serving in the army was reaching a record low. Staupers visited First Lady Eleanor Roosevelt at her New York apartment to discuss her plight. Although Mrs. Roosevelt made no promises, black nurses started to see some improvement in their experiences beginning in early 1945. In some instances black nurses were finally transferred out of POW camps.[9] In an anonymous letter to Mabel Staupers dated February 14, 1945, a chief nurse wrote, "I have heard very good news about the new assignments of colored nurses. They are no longer assigned only to P.W. camps. As you no doubt know those nurses who serve six months at these camps are rotated now to non P.W. camps."[10]

When they rotated after a six-month stint at a POW camp, the nurses usually ended up at a segregated base where they encountered whites-only and colored facilities, or at hospitals that had both POWs and Allied soldiers and which frequently expected black nurses to tend to German POWs whenever possible. Even the contingent of black nurses who traveled overseas that previous fall had been misled about their duties. Captain Mary L. Petty, a high-ranking African American officer, led a group of sixty-three black nurses to England in September 1944. Petty reportedly told the nurses that they had "come to foreign soil to render the greatest possible service in this theater and to do everything within its power to improve race relations."[11] Unbeknownst to them, however, the nurses had been sent to England to relieve a unit of white nurses as the hospital turned into one exclusively for prisoners of war. With ongoing shortages and wounded Allied men in desperate condition, it was agonizing for black nurses to be the military's go-to choice for POW care. Fortunately, after a few months, the army converted that particular hospital in England from a POW ward to a facility for Allied soldiers, which made the service of the black nurses who remained there into 1945 much more fulfilling.[12]

This minor improvement did nothing, however, to address the overall treatment of black nurses in the military. They still weren't utilized in large numbers and the army refused to give an adequate explanation.

In the spring of 1945, it was evident that Germany was losing badly, and Elinor and Frederick feared imminent separation. She knew that she could be transferred to another post at any moment. It was unheard of for a black nurse to want to stay in an isolating place like Florence, but Elinor remained there, so she must have assured her commanding officer that continuity of care was the most important thing and that she was fine continuing on in her post.

As the war approached its end, Frederick's status as a prisoner of war also hung in the balance. When Hitler committed suicide in April 1945, it was clear that Frederick had only so much time left in the United States. There was no way he would be allowed to stay in America as a German prisoner, and the possibility of his being allowed to walk out of the barbed-wire-enclosed camp and start fresh as an immigrant was particularly remote. His return to Germany was inevitable, but the idea of going back to an obliterated country where homes and businesses had been reduced to dust was incomprehensible to him and the other prisoners. Additionally, Frederick hadn't seen his family in years, and the thought of a reunion was complicated. He had no idea what his father would think of him as a returning POW— it's quite possible Karl Albert could have considered his son to be a coward for getting captured in the first place instead of fighting until the bitter end.

Elinor and Frederick remained at Florence through May 7, 1945, when Germany unconditionally surrendered to the Allied forces in Rheims, France. World War II was over and May 8, commonly known as VE Day for "Victory in Europe," became a public holiday marking the end of the Third Reich. Celebrations erupted around the world, and masses of people gathered in major cities, from Los Angeles to London, singing, crying, dancing, and celebrating in the streets.

It was a bittersweet time for Elinor and Frederick. Their future as a couple was in question, and they weren't prepared to live apart. In desperation, the two decided to seal their bond with an act that would unite them forever. As the months passed and the POWs were in the process of being transferred to temporary transitional camps before embarking on the transatlantic journey back to Europe, in April 1946, Frederick and Elinor made love in the hope of conceiving a child. As a nurse, Elinor knew about birth control and had access to it presumably from the moment she and

Frederick began an intimate relationship. But whatever pre-caution they had been taking to prevent a pregnancy was intentionally discarded.

They pledged their love to each other by attempting to bring a baby into the world to symbolize their union and commitment. They wanted to have a life together and de-cided that it would be easier for Frederick to get back into the United States if he were reuniting with his child.[13] It was a planned act of rebellion between two lovers, seen as soul mates by some, as silly fools by others.

Elinor was making the ultimate sacrifice to hold on to Frederick. She was putting her own future at serious risk. For one, she could not be pregnant and remain in the army. Further, once it became known that the father of her child was a "Nazi," which is how Frederick would be perceived regardless of what was in his heart, Elinor would face scorn, ridicule, possible unemployment, spinsterhood, and pov-erty. Also, although the war with Hitler was over, Jim Crow was not, and for a black woman to raise a mixed-race child would be challenging at best. She would endure prejudice and hatred from both sides, black and white.

Their unimaginable plan worked, and before Frederick left the United States Elinor was pregnant with his child. If there were tears, or cries of sadness and fear during their final moments together when they had to say good-bye at Camp Florence, the two kept those emotional details to themselves. But it would have been inconceivable for them if they hadn't felt a flood of heartache as they left each other's arms for the unknown. No one left war the same person. And Elinor and Frederick found a surreal love surrounded by millions of soldiers dying or returning home broken and maimed. Years later, in a rare admission, Elinor briefly spoke about the moment when the baby was conceived. Although she never revealed the location or date, or any specifics bordering on salacious, she did share with her son Chris when he was an adult that the passion between her and Frederick on that particular occasion—when they knew they had that one chance to bond themselves together for life—had been so intense that she was certain they had made a child, and in fact they had.

Elinor's final post in the United States Army Nurse Corps was at the Station Hospital in Fort Ord, near Monterey Bay, in California. She was placed on leave on September 12, 1946, and returned to Milton; with her army term officially ending on October 25, 1946. If Elinor was showing by the time she went on leave, there weren't any photos to prove it, and it's possible she concealed her pregnancy from the army. While in her second trimester, she could have fooled disinterested senior officers at Fort Ord about her condition by camouflaging a protruding stomach with oversized nurses' jackets and blaming her bulge on pure weight gain. But there would be no fooling Gladys Powell.

Elinor had no choice but to return home to Milton in what she knew to be the worst-case scenario in her mother's eyes: unmarried and pregnant with a German prisoner of war's baby. And Elinor would be living alone with her mother since her younger sister, Ruth, had moved to New York and her older sister, Gladys, had moved away years ago. Her pregnancy would be considered an embarrassment; it represented behavior not befitting a member of the Powell family, and she knew her mother would be furious. Gladys had grown up in Louisville, Kentucky, around the turn of the century, when the roots of Jim Crow were just taking hold, and she managed to earn a college degree and have a teaching career, followed by marriage to an upstanding army veteran from an admired family in Milton. Having a daughter return home from the war with a "baby out of wedlock," a phrase she would have used, would be enough to make her sick.

Elinor had no choice but to face her mother, along with any shaming that came her way. Deep down she knew she was strong enough to endure the admonishment. Frederick had promised to return to her, and that would get her through.

8.

An Uncertain Future

WHEN ELINOR AND FREDERICK WERE FORCED TO separate, with an ocean between them and nothing but a promise to reunite, the war had been over for more than a year and the United States was still in the muddled process of shipping thousands of German POWs back to Europe. Just as the prisoners had no idea what to expect when they first arrived in America as captured soldiers, they returned home with the same degree of uncertainty.

Hardly anyone was shocked when Germany surrendered. Even before Hitler killed himself on April 30, 1945, many had long since realized the war was lost. A poem written by a German POW at Camp Florence and translated into English represented the thoughts of despair shared by soldiers in the Wehrmacht in the final months of the war.

Christmas 1944

I hear not the bells of our Homeland ringing,
I see not the radiant hearts of the children at the Christmas tree,
The presenting of gifts with joy.

Oh, you terrible war, bringing misery,
shattering much happiness,
now Fate has exiled me in a strange land.

Do you know of the longing for our Homeland,
with forests of firs and snow-capped peaks?
So here we stand behind barbed wire, as fit as fir trees.
We sing Christmas songs, each ringing true,
because each is thankful for his life,
and wish that they bring greetings to our parents, brothers
     and sisters.
The hope stays again with us, enduring the love of our
     Homeland, again to see.[1]

The fatigue and weariness of living in captivity had pen-
etrated the minds of many prisoners. The U.S. military
monitored their morale throughout the war, either by in-
tercepting mail or by recording interactions between prisoners and American officers, which revealed a growing
consensus among U.S.-based POWs, especially during the
final months, that Hitler was a madman who needed to be
stopped. When FDR died on April 12, 1945, almost every
POW at Camp Florence reportedly added his signature to a

document to camp officials expressing condolences for the death of the U.S. president.[2]

Naturally there were prisoners who remained loyal to Hitler to the bitter end. One German POW, in captivity in an American camp in Europe, wrote in an intercepted letter, "The majority of us are confident that the Fuehrer will spare the Homeland from enemy intruders."[3] But that didn't happen, of course. And most German prisoners in the United States were relieved when the war came to an end.

Their relief was matched with fear and anxiety, however. Though longing to be reunited with loved ones, deep down the prisoners knew it was highly unlikely that they'd be able to resume the same lives they had led in Germany before the war. Instead, thousands wanted to stay in the United States to build new memories in a place that had become familiar and ripe with possibilities for a fresh start.

Rumors started to spread that they would be used as slave labor by the Russians, British, or French. The level of distress among the prisoners became so acute that there were reports of several thousand POWs wanting to volunteer to join the American army to help fight the Japanese.[4] They would learn, though, that under the Geneva Convention all prisoners had to be returned to their homelands.

POW camps began to close down as the facilities were converted for other purposes. Camp Florence would turn into a minimum-security prison and later a state hospital after it transferred out the POWs who had lived there.[5] Thousands of POWs moved to different camps throughout the United States before they left America for good. Many went to Camp Rupert in Idaho to harvest potatoes; others went elsewhere around the country to harvest fruit.[6]

The tenuous status of German POWs was exacerbated by the return of American soldiers, many wounded, who would need to recover and then find work. It was a complicated matter because certain factions wanted the POWs to remain in the United States and others wanted them gone. Labor unions, committed to the employment of American workers, wanted the German prisoners returned to Europe immediately, while farmers wanted to hold on to the cheap POW labor. Not only had they grown to depend on the Germans to tend to their farms, but an unexpected bond had developed, and a fair number of American farm families wanted the POWs to stay.[7] It was an emotional topic that the government did not want to see spiral out of control.

Some congressmen and senators argued emphatically that the POWs needed to leave the United States immediately and go home to Europe, where they could rebuild all the areas the Nazis had destroyed. Still, the farmers and industry leaders didn't back down. They insisted that low-wage prisoner of war labor had kept their farms and factories in business. Several politicians, indeed, discovered that even with the POWs, there was still a labor shortage—so these industries risked ruin if the prisoners departed immediately.[8]

Although it was unlikely that returning soldiers would feel threatened by jobs German POWs were doing, which were disparagingly referred to as "stoop-labor," the govern-ment could not risk having the public believe their loved ones would be competing with German POWs for jobs, no matter how remote the likelihood of such competition. Brigadier General B.M. Bryan, assistant provost marshal general, released a statement to emphasize the government's commitment to its soldiers. "We are not going to prevent any American from getting a job because of a prisoner. . . . If there's a civilian for the job he gets it."[9] But the truth was that no one had a clear-cut solution.

The War Department initially said it would first return the prisoners it deemed "useless," meaning the sick, the in-sane, and the unrepentant Nazis, but that announcement wasn't well received. Some Americans thought it wasn't fair for the hard-core ideological POWs to be able to leave cap-tivity so quickly and resume their lives back in Germany. "Genuine Nazis are being rewarded for their convictions with a speedy reunion with their families," according to a May 31, 1945 *New York Times* article.[10]

Moreover, the logistics of sending almost 400,000 Ger-man soldiers back to a battered and fragile Europe was daunting. There had been little guidance provided by the Geneva Convention about the return of prisoners in cir-cumstances of an "unconditional surrender." In place was a broadly worded provision in Article 75 stating that, "In any case, the repatriation of prisoners shall be effected as soon as possible after the conclusion of peace."[11] There were no firm deadlines, which gave the United States flexibility.

However, the continued care and guarding of POWs in Europe and the United States were unsustainable.

A decision was finally made to ship the POWs back as soon as possible. Between 1945 and 1948 the War Department staggered the return of prisoners, with the majority sent back to Europe during 1946. The speediness of their return was also motivated by President Truman's strategy, during a burgeoning Cold War, to strengthen ties with France and Britain, who desperately needed cheap POW labor to rebuild their bombed-out countries.[12] But that wasn't a smooth transition either.

Coordinating with the French and British was challenging, as both countries wanted to keep the POWs in captivity for as long as possible, in what sometimes turned out to be questionable and inhumane conditions, before finally releasing them. Article 75 of the Geneva Convention also stated, "Prisoners of war who are subject to criminal proceedings for a crime or offence at common law may, however, be detained until the end of the proceedings, and, if need be, until the expiration of the sentence. The same applies to prisoners convicted for a crime or offence at common law." With the loose wording, the French or Brits could accurately claim the destruction of their countries by the Nazis was both a crime and an offense, which meant their prolonged detainment of prisoners was not a violation.[13]

The American military government in Germany also preferred that the POWs be dispersed to other countries for the rebuilding efforts before returning home. In Germany there were food and fuel shortages, ravaged cities, and occupying forces. There was a real fear that POWs, upon returning home, would become disillusioned and resentful, starting uprisings and hindering efforts to establish peace. The War Department decided that some POWs would work in labor battalions in England and France, usually for six months but sometimes longer, and others would be repatriated directly to Germany—it was sheer luck which assignment a particular prisoner was given.[14]

For the journey back to Europe, POWs were given a barracks bag filled with blankets, a first-aid kit, and eating utensils. The government issued them checks, usually worth $50, or for POWs who had saved up more money from their work, a few hundred dollars. The prisoners took trains from their camps to the army's largest port of embarkation, which was at Camp Shanks, in Rockland County, New York. There they boarded vessels that usually carried three thousand prisoners across the Atlantic on a trip that lasted nine to ten days.[15]

Most vessels docked at Southampton, England, or Le Havre, France, off the English Channel. France held the German POWs the longest, possibly out of a combination of revenge and a genuine need for labor given the massive devastation the Nazis inflicted on the country during the war. Of the 700,000 German POWs France received from the combined European and American units, the French still had 440,000 under its authority in April 1947, almost two years after the war ended. And another 10,000 were still there in 1948.[16]

Unlike the German POWs who had been in captivity in Europe during the war, those who had been detained in the United States realized how comfortable their accommodations had been in comparison. At a camp in Hull, England, the prisoners lived in huts instead of barracks, and slept in bunk beds on straw sacks instead of mattresses. The hatred of Germans was palpable, and one report described a situation where prisoners who worked trimming hedges on a farm in the boiling sun had nothing offered to them but a dirty stream from which to drink water.[17]

Many of the POWs who were sent back to Germany couldn't believe the devastation. Some cities were unrecognizable. Instead of going immediately home to their loved ones, as they'd hoped, thousands of POWs lived in camps scattered across the country. At one in Münster, in northwest Germany, in the British zone, the POWs were forced to visit concentration camps.

The U.S. military had shown the prisoners detained in America film footage that the Allied forces had taken when they discovered the atrocities of the Holocaust. They wanted to see how the POWs would react. The responses varied; some wept, some held their heads low, others sat stoic. Many believed it was a manufactured propaganda film with actors. Some even thought the lifeless emaciated bodies were actually Germans who had been tortured and killed by the Russians. POW Friedrich Mögel, first detained in Arizona, then after the war, in Münster, was sent with other prisoners to the Dachau concentration camp outside of Munich. He was forced to stay there for two weeks to counter the false narrative that the camps weren't real. He was given his dismissal papers afterward.[18]

The exact date that Frederick left the United States isn't clear, but sometime after the baby was conceived in April 1946, he was sent back to Europe. Frederick's sister, Charlotte, said he was released to the British army and worked in a camp for approximately six months before returning home. The nature of his work and the details of the conditions he had to endure remain a mystery, with the exception of the bitter memory Frederick shared with Charlotte about being stripped of all his belongings by British soldiers upon entering the country. And like his fellow comrades who knew they were only a few days away from Germany by train, he just wanted his captivity to finally be over so he could begin to rebuild his life.[19]

Elinor hadn't lived in Milton since she left for nursing school in 1940, so her return after the war in early September 1946 would have been difficult under any circumstances. Almost six months pregnant and armed with nothing but a promise of Frederick's return, she was terrified at the thought of facing her mother and all that Milton represented. She later shared with her niece Hope Taylor that she knew her mother would think she had lost her mind. Frederick could have been lying about his feelings for her. Or maybe he would find the obstacles too great and decide to stay in Europe, never to reappear in the United States again and raise his child. But Elinor was convinced that he would keep his word.

Gladys's hypertension was serious. She mostly stayed in bed, but her weakened state didn't diminish her anger toward Elinor. As predicted, Gladys was furious about and embarrassed by her daughter's pregnancy. She was so disappointed she could barely look at Elinor, refusing to speak to her unless it was absolutely necessary.

Gladys was a very proud and religious woman. It was a major blight in her eyes to have Elinor return home pregnant and unmarried, and she worried about Elinor's reputation. The whole story seemed unfathomable to her even when Elinor told her that the pregnancy was planned. Tension permeated the house. With her strong personality, Gladys needed time to process the impending birth of her first grandchild.

Eventually Gladys turned a corner. The reality was that she put family before everything, and she decided that Elinor needed her support more than her scorn. Also, as a widow, she was lonely. She forgave Elinor for shaming the family and understood that her daughter was in a vulnerable situation and, frankly, desperate.[20]

When Stephen Albert was born in Boston on December 18, 1946, Gladys embraced him without any hesitation, falling in love with the cream-colored baby. She held her grandson as much as she could, and even while ailing, she lifted him up in her arms with an expression of sheer adoration—a moment that Elinor captured in a photograph glued in one of her cherished scrapbooks.

But what Gladys felt for her new grandson didn't translate

into any warmth for Frederick. She was convinced that he was nothing more than a hustler who had fooled her daughter into getting pregnant so he could get a sponsored visa, rather than remain in war-torn Germany, which everyone knew was in shambles. Gladys believed that the promises Frederick had made to Elinor about lasting love and marriage were just a slick way to gain entry into the United States.[21] But Elinor's trust in the father of her child never wavered.

Frederick knew he would return to Elinor, but he didn't know when and he didn't know how. He was also broke and hadn't been in regular contact with his parents since his conscription. He was bitter about his layover in the transitional camp in England, but after his stint was up, he returned to Austria.

Vienna had been spared heavy destruction compared to other major cities, particularly in Germany, and for a while during the war, Karl, Margarete, and Charlotte were able to make do with the bomb shelters in the basements of their apartment buildings until official shelters were built across the city. Charlotte remembered sweeping up dirt and pieces of glass scattered in the streets from the impact of the nearby air raids.

The devastation of the bombings changed landscapes entirely. By the end of the war, 75 percent of Germany had been severely bombed. More than 150 cities were decimated by air raids, with many repeatedly bombed into oblivion. The city of Kassel lost 10,000 civilians in a single night, on October 22, 1943, after an unrelenting series of bombs was unleashed by British warplanes. In Hamburg, more than 45,000 German residents died one July evening after a firestorm spread through the city. The number of German civilian deaths caused by Allied air raids alone was 600,000, and out of that, it was reported, 76,000 were children.[22]

Frederick moved in with Charlotte, who still had an intact apartment. Fortunately, it was in the American zone of Vienna, as opposed to the Russian zone, where she heard about people being robbed, raped, and killed by Soviet soldiers. She was divorced from her Austrian husband and had given her baby daughter, Kristina, to her parents to raise; Karl and Margarete had temporarily moved in with Margarete's sister in Siegen, Germany. Frederick relied on Charlotte completely and received food stamps provided by Allied occupying forces. Fortunately, he was able to resume his studies at the art academy while he figured out a way to return to Elinor.[23]

During this time, Frederick also started a brief romance with Charlotte's landlady. Back in the United States, Elinor gave no indication to anyone close to her that she and Frederick were in an open relationship. The plan, as far as she was concerned, involved doing everything possible to get her unofficial fiancé back on American soil. There were no discussions of dating other people, nor would such an arrangement work for Elinor given her compromised state. The fact was that Frederick was showing early signs of being a womanizer. He was capable of being romantically involved with two women simultaneously, a character trait he inherited from his father.[24] He also was twenty-one years old, with an uncertain future. He wanted nothing more than to marry Elinor—that decision was never in question—but how he would manage to move to America, build a life with her, and provide for their baby wasn't clear at all. The two lovers exchanged letters, with one written from Frederick to Elinor that she later glued into one of her scrapbooks. Worn with age, ink-smudged, and collaged with stamps and a large photo of Frederick, the readable parts reveal his devotion: "I need you terribly," "You are a part of me," "I can't let you wait so long," and "I love you."

Although Frederick did not remain faithful to Elinor during their separation, he loved her and remained committed to the idea of finding a way to get to the United States to be with her. Charlotte recalled that Frederick carried on with the landlady for months. And there wouldn't have been much Elinor could have done if she suspected the relationship. The option of raising a child on her own wasn't feasible considering how sick her mother had become. She really had nowhere to go; her future was riding on Frederick's return.

Frederick learned about his son's birth through a Western Union telegram: "EIGHT POUND SON BORN DECEMBER EIGHTEENTH MOTHER CHILD WELL. GLADYS POWELL." The very next day, Frederick telegraphed back, "BEST WISHES TO MOTHER AND CHILD LOVE FRIKA ALBERT." Although tersely worded, the telegrams were cherished mementos saved by both Elinor and Frederick and were later displayed proudly in one of Elinor's many scrapbooks.

Gwyneth Blessitt Moore stayed in the army after the war ended. Her family was in New York, and on a trip home she made her way farther north to see Elinor. Not much had changed in the army since their time together at Camp Florence. The end of the war hadn't altered race relations between whites and blacks in the military at all. It still functioned under Jim Crow, especially in the southern states. Gwyneth was stationed in Fort Bragg in North Carolina, which was a completely segregated base. There were separate barracks, hospitals, and recreational facilities for blacks and whites. "When we went to the movie theater, the black soldiers had to sit upstairs, and the whites downstairs," she recalled. Yet Gwyneth enjoyed her time at Fort Bragg because she met her husband there, an African American soldier who also was stationed at the post.

During one visit, Elinor asked Gwyneth to write a letter to the American consulate in Vienna in support of Frederick's immigration to the United States. She wanted her friend, who had been promoted to first lieutenant in the U.S. Army Nurse Corps, to provide a character endorsement of Frederick, along with proof of income to help out with Frederick's resettlement. Gwyneth obliged.

German immigration to the United States after the war was a complicated issue. Between 1820 and 1930, approximately six million Germans immigrated to the United States.[25] After World War II, with the United States emerging as the world's leading superpower, the nation had to get involved in the critical refugee crisis in Europe, and as an Allied occupying force, it also controlled Germany's migration policy. Germans looking for a better life sought out their American relatives for visa sponsorship, but there were firm travel restrictions placed on German citizens, making it very difficult for them to leave their occupied state. There was also a quota system that the United States still followed: the 1924 Immigration and Naturalization Act had established a yearly quota of 25,957 visas for Germans.[26]

Any chance of Germans immigrating to America after World War II rested on them belonging to preferred groups the U.S. government allowed for entry and sponsorship. With the threat of the Cold War and tensions rising between the Soviet Union and the United States, German rocket scientists were given visas, even those with Nazi ties. War brides of U.S. soldiers were given priority as well. Victims of National Socialism or close relatives of American citizens were also allowed to apply for visas but weren't guaranteed entry. The U.S. government required that immigrants from these groups have a sponsor to avoid dependence on social welfare programs. Sponsors, whether relatives, churches, volunteer organizations, or in some cases farmers who guaranteed housing and employment had to submit an affidavit pledging support of the immigrant. As a former POW, Frederick technically wasn't even allowed in the United States because anyone in the Wehrmacht couldn't reenter the United States until after September 1948, when the travel ban was lifted for Germans who didn't fall into any prioritized groups. But exceptions were always made, including for sponsored ex-POWs who posed no threat.[27] And in Frederick's case, he was a fiancé to Elinor and father to a newly born American son who needed his support.

Frederick's visa application was accepted, and Elinor saved a copy of the letter Gwyneth wrote. Her friend's generosity paid off, and Frederick was granted entry into the United States, arriving on June 21, 1947, and marrying Elinor five days later at the courthouse in downtown Manhattan.[28] The two saw no point in delaying their nuptials for any reason, and New York didn't have an anti-miscegenation law, like several other states in the United States, where their interracial marriage would have been against the law.

Elinor could finally silence all of the doubters about Frederick's love for her, her mother among them. He had come back and married her just as he had promised. And their nuptials helped bolster the less-than-flattering opinion Gladys initially had of her new son-in-law. From what she could tell, he did want to make a life in the United States, but as a husband and father, not as a hustler or manipulator.[29]

Elinor had endured nine months of pregnancy, much of that spent alone after Frederick was sent back to Europe, and another six months of single parenthood after Stephen's birth. But she was now Mrs. Frederick Albert. Gladys, bedridden, didn't witness the civil ceremony, but Hope Taylor, Elinor's niece, remembered hearing years later about an official celebration of Elinor's marriage back home in Milton. Even though Elinor defied all of the characteristics of a traditional bride, the etiquette that Gladys was accustomed to would have required a social gathering of some kind— one that was small and subdued given the extenuating circumstances, but a proper occasion nonetheless.

Although Gladys had a large-enough home, Elinor's relationship with her mother had always been fragile, and Elinor most likely thought it was better to start fresh somewhere else. The young couple and their child stayed at Ruth's place temporarily in New York when they first married, but a family of three could overstay their welcome within days, so Frederick took odd jobs to make enough money to find a place of their own.

If they were outraged by Frederick's decision to return to America for a black woman, Karl and Margarete didn't voice it to Charlotte. The story of how they learned of their son's decision isn't clear. Once he was back in Vienna he could have called or written to his parents about his plans, but that part of the story is unknown to surviving relatives. Chris Albert, born years after Stephen, even wondered with amusement about how his father broke the news about Elinor. "Did he say, 'Now I'm going to go back to America because she's pregnant' or 'because I love her,' or 'Oh, by the way she's black and about six feet tall'? Who knows what." [30]

There were always gaps in communication and unshared moments within the Albert family. Charlotte was barely in touch with her parents even though they were raising her daughter. The war only intensified the difficult dynamics in this already emotionally fractured family.

Whatever Frederick did or did not reveal to his parents didn't alter his decision—that much is clear. Elinor and Frederick's precarious plan to bring him back to the United States had worked. They were living together as a family. But they hadn't thoroughly considered how they were going to raise their son, or where'd they live or work. When they got married, Frederick was almost twenty-two and Elinor twenty-six and neither had spent much time functioning in the real world as independent adults. Their entire lives had been structured for them—first by their parents, then by their schooling, and finally by their respective armies. Neither Frederick nor Elinor had lived on their own, really, let alone as a mixed-race couple with a baby who was half German and half African American. They were sure of their devotion to each other, but it is unlikely that they understood just how much and how frequently that love would be tested.

9.

Searching for Acceptance

ALTHOUGH THE MARRIAGE CERTIFICATE LISTED Frederick's official name as Friedrich, at some point the couple decided to Americanize his name, and he became known to everyone as Frederick or by his nickname, Frika. Elinor and Frederick's relationship was now out in the open for the first time since they had met. Emotions ran high as everyone tried to adjust to postwar life, but Elinor took comfort in being a married woman. She was unfazed that Frederick was white, and she wanted to put behind her the discrimination that she had endured in the army.

For the nurses who remained in the U.S. Army Nurse Corps after the war, a moment of progress arrived at last. The determination and activism of Mabel Staupers, the NAACP and other civil rights groups, the Negro press, and Eleanor Roosevelt eventually paid off when President Truman banned segregation in the U.S. Army and Navy in 1948. Executive Order 9981 stated, "There shall be equality of treatment and opportunity for all persons in the armed services without regard to race, color, religion or national origin."[1]

A few years later, in 1951, Mabel Staupers dissolved the National Association of Colored Graduate Nurses and folded its membership into the American Nurses Association, the very organization that for decades had denied black nurses entry. Staupers felt the goal of the NACGN had been met now that the ANA had to admit all qualifying nurses regardless of race and now that, by law, black women were able to serve in the U.S. Army and Navy without any quotas or restrictions.[2]

American society, however, had not evolved as quickly and was not prepared to deal with a couple like Elinor and Frederick. They did not exactly fade into the background: she was a tall, statuesque African American woman and a former army nurse; he was a handsome, reserved former German soldier. After marrying in New York, they decided to move to Boston, where Elinor thought they'd have a better chance to find affordable housing and low-skilled employment for Frederick.

They chose Roxbury, a no-frills working-class neighborhood populated mostly by families crammed into small apartments. The housing market was tight with the return of veterans and the baby boom. But Elinor and Frederick faced an even greater challenge. There were plenty of people who still harbored bitter feelings about the war and who thought all Germans were "Nazis" or "Krauts." Moreover, some landlords weren't thrilled about renting an apartment to a German with a black wife and mixed-race baby. Elinor and Frederick would end up moving frequently, mostly because neighbors complained to landlords about living next to them and threatened to move.[3]

Elinor and Frederick stayed the longest in an attic apartment where they met an African American dentist, Edward Allen, who had served in the U.S. Navy and who would become a good family friend. Allen's tiny apartment was across from theirs, and he remembered them as a loving couple who kept to themselves.[4]

The late Senator Edward Brooke, who was a Boston lawyer then, lived nearby and heard about Frederick. He sought him out because he needed some documents translated from German to English, and the two became friends. They had much in common as two veterans of the war, although from opposite sides. Brooke, who was African American, had been an officer in the segregated 366th Infantry Regiment. When his unit went to Italy, he fell in love with and married an Italian woman, and they had two children.[5]

Frederick's career was on a far less promising course than that of his distinguished friend with political ambitions. Frederick worked all hours of the night at a bakery, which gave him very little time to socialize and acquaint himself with neighbors. The hours at the bakery were unforgiving—he had to wake up early in the morning to get the fresh bread out, and he struggled to make ends meet.

It was a low-skilled job and the situation was stressful for Elinor, whose anxiety was already escalated by the passing of her mother in May 1948 of a cerebral hemorrhage.[6]

Gladys Farrow Powell had been very ill for years, but it was still a blow when the matriarch passed away at age fifty-two. The town of Milton mourned too; as previously noted, in her obituary Gladys was lauded for her role as a leader in the Girl Scouts. She had been the highest-ranking African American in a leadership position in the entire organization.[7]

With her two sisters living their own lives in different states, and both parents now gone, Elinor had to make her new family work without any of the support she had grown accustomed to having. She and Frederick had a child to raise and no money. Neither one of them had ever really known what it was like to worry about finances, because both of their families had prospered. Renting a cramped attic apartment was a frightening reality, and at some point Elinor and Frederick both realized they were on a path to poverty. They would not be able to buy their own house at the rate they were going, and given how society felt about mixed-race couples, getting a mortgage would have been extremely difficult even if they had the means.

After a few years of scraping by in Boston, living in dilapidated apartments, Elinor suggested they move to Germany to live with Frederick's family. By then, Karl had a new engineering company that was doing well. And there was nothing keeping Elinor in Boston anymore—after her mother's death, she and her sisters sold the house on Emerson Road—and she felt like she was at a crossroads. She never wanted Frederick to resent moving to America for her, and she knew enough about his background to understand that he was sacrificing a great deal to start over with nothing just to be with her. She also knew a life of poverty in Boston was not what they had dreamed about when they mapped out their lives as young lovers at Camp Florence.[8]

Frederick was hesitant. He was resistant to the idea of relying on his parents for anything, and he and Elinor would be moving to Germany with nothing more than the clothes on their backs, which meant they would have no choice but to live with his parents while he worked for his father. Frederick had no idea how his parents would receive his new family, and although he had suppressed his longing for his father's approval, he knew that if he returned to Germany he risked falling back into a trap of rejection.

After much back-and-forth, Frederick finally agreed to the move with one caveat: he would give it one year. If they weren't happy in Germany after that, they would return to the United States immediately. He decided to be cautiously optimistic about working for his father's company because he would finally be able to provide for his family of three. He also knew that, as the only son, he was the natural choice for taking over his father's business one day, which would help his parents warm to the idea of his move back to Germany to live with them. He would be groomed to be the next CEO, which would mean a significant upgrade to his current lifestyle. If his parents knew he and his family had been living in a shabby attic apartment, they would have been ashamed.

It wasn't just Frederick's anxiety about working for Karl that gave him pause. He knew his parents still believed in the German empire. With the fall of the Third Reich and for survival reasons in occupied territory, no one in Germany still openly supported Nazism after the war. However, his parents were German nationalists, and that strong national pride came with feelings of racial superiority. Frederick couldn't guarantee Karl and Margarete would accept his new black family.

Elinor didn't let that dissuade her. As far as she was concerned, his parents' opinions couldn't have been worse than what she had endured living in Arizona. With the same optimism, devotion, and determination they had exhibited at Camp Florence and while they waited to be reunited from across the ocean, Elinor and Frederick began to pack for Germany.[9]

On August 1, 1952, Elinor, Frederick, and five-and-a-half-year-old Stephen boarded the TSS *Neptunia*, a passenger liner sailing from Boston to Bremerhaven, Germany.

Life had irrevocably changed everywhere in Europe after World War II. Even before the war ended, Margarete and Karl had been reduced to using food ration cards just like every other Austrian and German who survived the collapse of Nazism. Toward the final months of the war, fearful of bombing, they left their apartment in Vienna and retreated to a home in the Austrian countryside that Charlotte claimed her father had previously shared with a mistress.

That he was a German officer in the reserves made Karl a prime target for reprisals in Vienna after the war, undoubtedly adding to the decision to leave Austria permanently. Even though Austria was once part of the Third Reich and took part in Nazi atrocities, the country's narrative after Germany's defeat became that of a victim of a brutal dictatorship, not that of a collaborator.

With territories redrawn, millions of Europeans would have no choice but to live elsewhere—mandates implemented by British, French, American, and Russian occupation forces, which needed to control and keep track of displaced populations. Charlotte even kept her mother's Allied Expeditionary Force DP Index Card, the ID the Allied governments gave to displaced persons during the war. The card provided serial numbers that allowed governments to track people who were being resettled. After their temporary stint in Siegen, Karl and Margarete moved to Vogelbeck, in Lower Saxony, Germany, where Karl started another company. He didn't sit back and wait for Germany to figure out its next steps as an occupied and battered nation. He loved working, being in charge, and making money too much, and he quickly figured out a way to profit from the country's rebuilding efforts.

His new company in Vogelbeck was called Feuerfest, later renamed Refratechnik. It developed refractory bricks made of slag from the steel and iron industries. Soon Karl had acquired enough money from contracts to move the factory to nearby Göttingen and build a beautiful house, in which he, Margarete, and Charlotte's daughter, Kristina, were able to live quite comfortably.[10]

Elinor and Frederick were naive about the climate of post–World War II Göttingen, and would soon discover it wasn't a congenial place for a mixed-race couple. Their primary concern was that Karl and Margarete had the means to house them and provide employment for Frederick, and that Kristina could be a playmate for Stephen.

Göttingen had been spared the structural damage from bombings that most other German cities suffered during the war. It was a university town in a valley along the Leine River, just south of Hanover. Göttingen was conservative in values and politics, and renowned for being the home of Georg-August University, founded in 1737, which was also the city's largest employer. The university was one of Europe's leading institutions for science and mathematics and churned out a substantial number of Nobel laureates in the twentieth century. By all accounts, the town's citizens had embraced Adolf Hitler and the Nazi Party.[11]

Despite the presence of a university, which usually would include a population of forward-thinking scholars, Göttingen favored right-wing ideas over left-wing ones, particularly during Hitler's rise to power in the 1930s, when the Hitler Youth, SA, and SS were embraced by the community. Like in other German towns during the Third Reich, the small population of Jews was persecuted in Göttingen.

Professors at the university were forced to leave and the local synagogue was burned down in 1938. Denazifying the city after the war wasn't going to be a quick transformation.[12]

For Frederick and Elinor, moving in with Karl and Margarete brought with it a host of uncertainties. Not only would Frederick be introducing his non-German-speaking African American wife and son to his non-English-speaking parents for the first time, but they would all be living under the same roof.

Frederick's communication with his parents had been just short of nonexistent during the war. Charlotte remembered that the family did receive one letter informing them that he had been taken to the United States as a prisoner of war, but they had no contact after that. Frederick hadn't spent any significant length of time with Margarete and Karl in years. Many unpalatable scenarios could have resulted from the move, but Elinor reassured Frederick that it was better to test the situation rather than look back with regret. More than anything, she never wanted him to struggle in the United States wondering what could have been and to resent her for denying him a chance to run his father's company.[13]

Karl and Margarete's home in Göttingen was a definite upgrade in sophistication and size from Elinor and Frederick's Boston accommodations. "The house was very beautiful," said Kristina. "It was newly built according to the plans and wishes of my grandmother, quite modern for the fifties." What Margarete designed was a two-story white stucco home that included a small goldfish pond and a large garden that she spent countless hours tending. The home's interior, grand and airy with sizable windows, had a formal yet comfortable aesthetic. The living areas included large velvet sofas in green and gold, and dark hardwood floors covered with soft carpets. Large crystal chandeliers adorned the main entertaining areas. There was a two-room suite in the back of the house where Frederick, Elinor, and Stephen would live.

The dedicated space allowed for privacy for both families, which one would assume was a thoughtful arrangement, but from the moment Frederick and Elinor arrived, they realized that the separate quarters were more isolating than considerate.

Karl and Margarete had never been in any intimate setting with black people before, and they truly weren't ready for the adjustment. They had not digested what it would mean to have not one but two non-Aryans living with them. The only exposure Germans had had to African Americans in recent years was during the occupation of Germany when black soldiers from the United States and the British Army's Caribbean regiments were stationed there. Before World War II, there had been a minuscule population of Africans who had moved to Germany to teach African languages during the country's colonial period in the early twentieth century. There were also black scholars and entertainers from all over the world who had spent time there.

Some had intimate relationships with German women, as did some of the French-African occupying soldiers in Germany after World War I. This small population of blacks, as well as the mixed-race children from these unions, although rarely acknowledged, ended up being victims of Hitler's barbarism in addition to Jews and other groups deemed inferior. Some fled before Nazism spread across the country, but others weren't as lucky and were sent to concentration camps and sterilized.[14]

Despite the fact that black GIs had a presence in Germany during the years-long occupation after World War II, it was unheard of for a German soldier to return from the war with an African American wife and mixed-race child. Interracial coupling was still very much a taboo. It was more common for a black man to take up with a white woman, and there were frequent reports and complaints to the U.S. military about love affairs between black GIs and local German women in some of the larger cities that had American military bases, such as Stuttgart and Frankfurt.

Elinor and Frederick were entering a country where interracial dating, marriage, and children were still isolated experiences that were scorned by German society. During the Allied occupation from 1947 to 1955, an estimated 67,000 children were born to soldiers from the occupied forces and German women. Out of that, a reported 4,776 were "brown babies." That term and *mischlingskinder* were used to describe mixed-race children with white German mothers and black fathers. The ostracizing of these children would have been a good indication for Frederick and Elinor of what was in store for them had they known.

Mischlingskinder were often placed in orphanages because no German families wanted to raise a half-black child. The children were seen as a blight on German culture and were mistreated. In response to the terrible predicament of these unwanted tan-skinned babies, an African American journalist named Mabel Grammer intervened. Grammer was married to Oscar Grammer, a black warrant officer stationed in Mannheim, Germany, from 1950 to 1954. She became aware of the discrimination these mixed-raced children faced when she was approached by German women seeking her help and nuns overseeing orphanages. She came up with the "Brown Baby Plan," a transatlantic adoption program that placed mixed-race children in Germany who were in need of good African American families to adopt them. France, England and Italy were also facing a similar crisis where babies born to black soldiers and European white women were shunned and unwanted. The October 1948 cover of *Ebony* magazine pictured a mixed-race baby with the headline "Homes Needed for 10,000 Brown Orphans." [15]

The shunning of these mixed-race babies was emblematic of how both German and American society felt about black-white romantic relationships. German women who had children fathered by black soldiers were treated as castaways and had very few options for maintaining a decent life as a single parent without harassment and constant threats.

Even though America was by no means free of racial prejudice, Mabel Grammer believed the orphans would be better off in the United States. It was no secret that the "brown babies" were leaving one oppressive regime, the remnants of the Third Reich, for another, Jim Crow, but Grammer thought that at least the children would have loving black families to take care of them. There would be communities of African Americans that would rally behind these children, unlike in Germany, where there was no significant black population.

As the occupation continued into the 1950s, so did the relationships between black soldiers and German women. But they fraternized at their own peril. Blacks in uniform found themselves on the receiving end of the same indignities experienced in the United States, and by the same oppressors: white Americans. When German women were caught on dates with black men, they were reportedly called "nigger-whores" by Americans in uniform. These women were often harassed on the street and even threatened with incarceration. One black soldier stationed in the European theater, when interviewed by NAACP president Walter White, reportedly said, "What are we fighting for over here? Are we sent . . . to fight the Nazis—or our white soldiers?" [16]

The U.S. military was aware of the injustices that white

soldiers inflicted on black soldiers. In just one of many examples, in 1946, Dwight D. Eisenhower received a letter from Alvin M. Owsley, "an indignant former national commander of the American Legion," after he saw a picture of a black GI and a white German woman. Owsley wrote:

> My dear General, I do not know . . . where these negroes come from, but it is certain that if they expect to be returned to the [U.S.] South, they very likely are on the way to be hanged or burned alive at public lynchings by the white men of the South. . . . There is only one way to stop the white man of the South from burning and hanging blackmen who lay their hands on our white women and that is . . . [for] . . . the blackmen to associate with black women and leave our women alone.[17]

Black men stationed in Germany endured verbal slurs and physical threats. If a black soldier was spotted walking alongside a German woman, uniformed white soldiers were known to drive their vehicles onto the sidewalks as if they were about to run the black GI down. Sometimes these threats led to actual violence. In Asberg, Bavaria, white GIs threw beer bottles at black servicemen dancing with German women. A brawl later ensued, and a white soldier was fatally shot. Three black soldiers were court-martialed and sentenced to hang.[18]

The strife between black and white American soldiers signaled to Germans that racism against blacks was acceptable. For example, there were alleged acts of discrimination by store owners who refused to serve black soldiers or their families. Some German bar owners, under pressure from white American GIs, barred black soldiers from their establishments. Anticipating objection from black GIs, white military police would patrol outside the bars in case any black soldiers attempted to enter.[19]

If that treatment had been directed at a white soldier, there would have been repercussions. But since blacks were on the receiving end, the slights went unpunished and excused. Ironically, Germans learned from their American occupiers that white supremacy was a shared value in both American and German cultures.

The town of Göttingen was completely unprepared for Elinor. Her time there was reminiscent of the days she spent being turned away from soda counters in Arizona. She was in a hostile environment. As an American, and a black American at that, her presence was an immediate reminder of the failed German empire and of a world that was forever changed.

Kristina Brandner, Charlotte's oldest daughter, was living with Karl and Margarete when Frederick, Elinor, and Stephen arrived. She was almost ten years old and fascinated with Elinor, the first black woman she had ever seen. Because she attended schools in the British zone, she could speak English.

Kristina was raised similarly to Frederick and Charlotte. The war had not softened anything about Margarete or

Karl's reserved temperament toward children. Even after the devastation of World War II, there was a coldness that remained in the Albert household. Instead of being the grandchild that everyone doted on, Kristina wasn't showered with kisses, hugs, and compliments. She experienced the same loneliness growing up as her mother and Frederick had.

"My grandparents were very strict. I had to learn good manners, discipline. They weren't open-minded," said Kristina.

When Elinor arrived, the dynamic in the house immediately shifted. For one, "Frika" was finally home, and Margarete was thrilled to have her favorite child back. To see him fawn over Elinor was difficult for her to watch, though. She was jealous of the attention Frederick gave his wife, and the fact that she was black made it even worse.

Elinor's race was an undeniable issue for Margarete. She couldn't grasp that she and a black woman were on equal footing. Kristina remembered Margarete saying that as a German woman, she couldn't relate to Elinor, because her only familiarity with blacks came from photos of Africans in books wearing tribal garb. "That's all my grandmother knew."

The lingering effects of German nationalism were very present in the Albert household. To Margarete, Elinor belonged to a foreign race. Kristina also attributed Margarete's discomfort with Elinor to Hitler's ban on foreign newspapers, which had made it illegal to provide information about other countries to German citizens. Margarete knew nothing at all about African Americans. Knowing Elinor couldn't understand her, Margarete constantly asked Kristina, "How come Frika couldn't marry someone white?"[20]

If Elinor thought she would bond with her new mother-in-law, she was mistaken. There wasn't anything Elinor could do right in Margarete's eyes. Kristina remembered how her grandmother acted: "She wanted to tell Elinor how to do everything and what not to do." The admonishments came in the form of shouting, which hurt Elinor deeply, but she was living in Margarete's house, so she had no choice but to deal with the frequent screaming, which was, of course, in German. "Elinor suffered a lot. I saw the fights," said Kristina.

Margarete even frowned upon Elinor buying fashion magazines, which Margarete thought were a waste of money and nothing more than frivolous expenses. The reprimand had an undercurrent of shaming because it implied that Elinor was ungrateful and spent money carelessly. Margarete had always maintained a regular beauty regimen. She would get manicures every week and a pedicure once a month. She visited the hair salon weekly for her signature look, a low chignon.[21] Instead of seeing Elinor's interest in fashion and design as a common bond the two could share, however, she chastised her daughter-in-law about her shallowness. Although Elinor usually couldn't understand what her mother-in-law was saying until Kristina translated, her combative tone was enough to ascertain the meaning of her words.

"Elinor was so unhappy and my grandmother could yell, my God, she could yell." said Kristina. "Sometimes I went after Elinor. I saw her in the kitchen in the morning crying. How could she be happy here?"

Elinor did her best to adapt to her inhospitable mother-in-law because she had a son to raise, but she mostly retreated to the suite that she and Frederick occupied. "I felt very badly for Elinor," said Kristina. "My grandmother did not like her and didn't want her there. To her, Frika married this *black* woman."[22] That infuriated Margarete. She didn't understand how her son could choose someone black over someone white. And word spread quickly about the new "black woman" and tan child living with the Alberts.

Elinor couldn't leave the house without gawkers following her. What should have been an uneventful stroll down Wenderstrasse often turned into a spectacle. Everyone stared at Elinor wherever she went. One man, coming out of a store, dropped his bag of groceries when he saw her, and stood there motionless as his cabbage rolled down the sidewalk. Charlotte, on a visit, was with Elinor at the time. "He acted as if he had been struck by lightning. I'll never forget that episode."[23] It's quite possible that Elinor was the first black person most residents of Göttingen had ever seen up close. That, coupled with her statuesque six-foot physique and striking dark skin, shocked people into paralysis.

It was unnerving for Elinor to stand out in this way. She felt as though she was a walking exhibit or an animal in a zoo, but she had no choice but to leave the house because little Stephen had to go to school and play outside. The two of them together stirred up so much curiosity and resentment that Kristina found herself in the unfortunate position of constantly answering questions about her aunt as well as her cousin, who looked neither white nor black.

"In school, the other kids used to ask me how come there was a black woman living with us. 'And your cousin, why is he another color?' " On some occasions, Kristina remembered, the children in her neighborhood would yell "nigger" when Elinor or little Stephen walked outside.

Despondent and humiliated, Elinor couldn't even give rude and obnoxious finger-pointing people a piece of her mind. She didn't pick up German easily, so she wasn't able to communicate with anyone. She was lonely and frustrated, not unlike when she first moved to Camp Florence. Kristina remembered that Elinor was alone all the time. "She had no friends. Nobody to talk to. Now that I'm a grown woman I can understand and feel what she felt." [24]

It wasn't just Elinor who was miserable. Frederick was suffering too. The truth was that he was not succeeding in his father's company. From the moment he arrived, he couldn't adjust to the work—developing fireproof products. He was not the least bit interested in manufacturing and engineering. It was too technical and the experience was not bringing him any closer to his father.

Kristina, even as a child, found it disturbing that Frederick didn't defend Elinor when Margarete was mistreating her. It had to have been even more disappointing for Elinor to watch Frederick retreat instead of sticking up for her. But Frederick avoided any confrontation with Margarete. He just relegated himself to his suite with his tiny family. He didn't have any friends in Göttingen either. The home was fraught with tension, and the two families lived separate lives under one roof.

"We very rarely had family meals together," said Kristina. "My grandmother cooked for my grandfather, herself, and me. And Elinor cooked separately for her family. We ate at different times and in different rooms: Elinor, Frika, and Stephen in their part of the house and we in the dining room."[25] Occasionally the two families would take Sunday walks together, but that didn't happen often. And Karl, who would later be diagnosed with Parkinson's disease, never joined them for their strolls but not because of his health; he had taken up with a new girlfriend and preferred to spend his weekends with her.

Frederick was in a difficult situation. He was living with his wife and child in his family home, which was safe and comfortable despite his parents' inhospitable treatment. He was beholden to his father for employment, knowing he would be at the helm of the company one day even though he hated the work he was doing and the business he would eventually own. It seemed as though the practical aspects of his life—steady housing and income—were both severely compromised by the degree of unhappiness that came along with them. Yes, his parents were sparing him from a life of destitution in Boston, but the very things he feared about the move had come to fruition. He wasn't thriving at his job, his father still didn't embrace him, and his mother didn't accept his wife.

Elinor later shared with her niece Hope Taylor that when she lived in Göttingen, she had to double-check the word for "black" in German because that's how often Margarete would say it. She told Hope that one time she could hear her mother-in-law telling someone on the phone that she had a "nigger" in her house.[26]

It was a hopeless situation for Elinor. She was on her own while Frederick worked. The only time she had adult conversation was when he returned from the office. She picked up as much pidgin German as she could and learned to cook Bavarian food on her own to pass the time. She eventually would make excellent German meals—but it wasn't because Margarete taught her.

The move to Germany turned out to be terrible. Frederick and Elinor had a nice place to live, but that was the only improvement in their lives. It was inevitable that Elinor became depressed in such an alienating environment. It was becoming clear that she couldn't stay there for much longer.

A part of her still wanted to believe that she and Frederick could make it work for financial reasons. And Elinor soon discovered she was pregnant with their second child. The two knew, though, that their marriage was suffering. "I think Elinor would have left Frika had they remained in Germany," said Charlotte. Frederick realized that too. He was in love with his wife and he hated seeing her unhappy.

Instead of fighting with his mother or demanding more respect from his father, he would leave. That was what he and Elinor had agreed on before they left the United States. Moving was becoming a survival mechanism for them. If wherever they landed didn't work out, they would pack up and venture to a new destination.

After a year in Göttingen, their second son, Christopher Wilhelm Farrow Albert, was born on June 17, 1953. Shortly thereafter, Frederick and Elinor decided to move back. The lure of family wealth didn't outweigh their love for each other. Frederick would have to figure out a way to make the United States work, even though he hadn't been successful the first time. He had to get Elinor out of Germany.

10.

Finally Home

FREDERICK DECIDED IT WOULD BE BEST TO RE-turn to the United States ahead of Elinor and the children. He wanted to find a job and a suitable place to live before sending for his family. It would have been difficult to search for housing with two young children in tow. And the truth was that it was easier to get a lease without the landlord and neighbors seeing his black wife and biracial sons.

If there was one positive takeaway from their time in Göttingen, it was that they would never have to wonder, "What if?". Frederick had gained the clarity he needed on many poignant levels. He now had proof that he could not comfortably and peacefully live in Germany with his African American wife and two mixed-race sons. The community in Göttingen wasn't ready to accept his nontraditional family. And the move was further confirmation that Frederick could never work for his father and be happy. The two men would never be close. Frederick had tried again and failed—a hurtful reality, but one that gave him closure on the matter. The truth was that Germany wasn't home to Frederick anymore, which meant the United States had to be. And Frederick was determined to make this move a good one for his family.

He applied for all kinds of odd jobs, mainly blue-collar. Although he was still passionate about art, his work experience was mostly in bakeries and most recently in his father's factory. He temporarily lived in Philadelphia at the YMCA on Arch Street. It was a humbling experience to be reduced to transient housing, but Frederick had set his ego aside when he left Germany. His luck changed on August 11 when he received a Western Union telegram to report for a training program at Piasecki Helicopter Company in Morton, Pennsylvania, outside of Philadelphia. His experience working in the engineering field with machinery at his father's company had paid off. He was instructed to bring his birth certificate and army discharge papers on his first day. It was a mechanic position, but Frederick didn't care. The job would allow him to earn enough money—combined with the small amount of money he had saved in Germany while living in his parents' house—to bring his family back to the States. Two months later, on October 6, 1953, Elinor and the children boarded a transatlantic vessel in Cuxhaven, Germany, to sail to New York, leaving Europe behind for good.

Frederick had found a modest rental house in the Philadelphia suburbs and he bought a used Saab. Elinor settled into her role as a stay-at-home mom, albeit begrudgingly, while Frederick worked nonstop, often two jobs, as the sole breadwinner. They could have used her additional income, but Frederick insisted that Elinor remain at home. He believed that a wife and mother should oversee the running of the household and take care of the children while the husband provided for the family. He didn't want her to be a career nurse, and he preferred to work late-night shifts at a bakery rather than have his wife work at all.[1]

One of the many things that Elinor made Frederick feel, from the moment he met her, was that he was needed, and he relished that feeling. She played a role in creating a dynamic in which she was very much the recipient and Frederick the provider who would see that she had everything she needed both emotionally and materially. If Elinor had to contribute to the family's household, then Frederick's role as the one true provider would be compromised, and he couldn't afford to give that up. The damage done by his relationship with his father created a vulnerability within him that would not have been able to withstand this blow.

Elinor, rather than protesting, focused on getting her children acclimated to American life. She certainly wasn't going to push Frederick on the idea of working. Göttingen had been her idea, and although her husband had agreed, the move was a painful failure. Elinor felt responsible for the heartache Frederick had endured because of his parents, and she wanted something to be easy and positive for him. She decided that thing would be their relationship. Frederick's ego had taken a tremendous blow in Germany, and she wanted to reassure him that their love, their union, would always be her number one priority.

She also wanted to get her children into a routine. Christopher was still in diapers, but because they had returned in October, school was already in session and Stephen needed to be enrolled immediately. He was almost seven years old and would have to adjust once again to a new city, a new house, and a new school where he would have to make new friends. Elinor and Frederick decided on the Sidney Smedley School, an elementary school close to where they lived.

Elinor, always impeccably groomed, dressed Stephen in smart school clothes and headed to the Smedley School for what she thought would be a routine enrollment process. She was eager to get her son back into the American school system. But Stephen didn't get enrolled that day, and the reasons were revealed in a scathing letter Elinor wrote to the Morton School Board. A copy, showing wear and tear, was saved by Elinor and glued into one of her scrapbooks.

Our family has moved recently to Morton, after our arrival in October of this year, we took our son to the nearest elementary school, The Smedley School, for admission. We spoke to the principal, who in seeing that the child was a Negro, advised us that the Phyllis Wheatley School, within the same district was the school for him. Our questions as to why this was necessary resulted only in a maint[ena]nce of her stand and a referral to the School Board if further clarification was desired. In order not to prolong my son's

already overdue enrollment that we placed him in the suggested "Negro" school a couple blocks away and later pre-
sented the matter to the School Board at its next meeting.
By the time we had looked up the law pertaining to segregation in Pennsylvania and had learned that it specifically
forbids "any discrimination whatever on account of or by
reason of race or color of any pupil seeking admission
"to any public school." My request to The School Board,
therefore, was that the law to be adhered to. It was disillu-
sioning to be advised that a special meeting of the Board
members would be required to "decide," and that I would
be informed of the result. In view of the existing law, it
is not clear to me what there is to decide but I will wait.

This is the situation my family faced in returning to
the United States after a year in Europe. Our home there
was in the British zone of Germany, and our son, a for-
eigner, was enthusiastically and unrestrictedly welcomed
in an English school. As an American citizen, in his own
country, such was not the case.

The Supreme Court of the United States is at present
deciding the constitutionality of segregated schools and
wide scale concern is given to the effect of integration in
Ala., Miss., and Georgia. Now I ask can we ever consider
harmony in these openly opposing states when here in
Pennsylvania where democracy and the Constitution was
born, is it so passively practiced?[2]

Elinor E. Albert

For Elinor, her child's denial of admission was similar to the humiliating slights she had experienced in her own life. The segregation at Camp Florence and the degrading encounters in Göttingen were similar to the discrimination being directed at her son. The message was that Stephen didn't belong in a white school because he was black, just like Elinor didn't belong in white establishments because of the color of her skin. It became increasingly clear that racism followed Elinor wherever she went—Boston, Göttingen, and now Philadelphia. It was infuriating, unlawful, and personal.

Elinor sent a copy of her letter to the local chapter of the NAACP in Media, Pennsylvania, which in turn responded:

Dear Mrs. Albert,

The Media Branch NAACP wishes to take this opportunity to commend you for the courage you possessed in taking your stand with the Morton School Board. Needless to say it is very necessary that we have more parents with such courage and faith as you.

> Sincerely Yours,
> Josephine L. Shumate
> secretary [3]

Elinor kept tabs on the Morton school board even though Stephen never attended the Smedley School. In the same scrapbook as her letter, she included a dateless clip about the school district from a local newspaper with the headline "Morton Expects Integration by Next Autumn."

Elinor and Frederick did their best to shield their sons from bigoted people, but they couldn't prevent it entirely. Nor did they fully grasp how being mixed-race impacted their sons' lives. One afternoon Elinor found Stephen yelling out the window, "Nigger, nigger," to a black child he saw outside on the street. She grabbed him immediately and pulled him away, but she knew why he was doing that. He was repeating what he had been called by the children in Göttingen. He was simply imitating what he had experienced himself.[4]

It could only have been shocking for Elinor to see how her son had been affected by some of the decisions she and Frederick had made, including moving to Germany. Yet Elinor and Frederick didn't complain to family members about the discrimination they encountered. Whenever something happened, Elinor and Frederick moved—that was their survival mechanism. Focusing on prejudice could have destroyed their relationship, since it seemed the world was against them. Instead, Elinor and Frederick put things behind them and left them there.

When Frederick wanted to purchase life insurance he made several calls to schedule an appointment. Well-dressed men in suits would stop by their house, but a disturbing pattern of rejection ensued. Once the agents arrived and discovered Frederick was married to a black woman, they would go through the pretense of showing him different insurance options but would then deny him coverage each time. At one point, a salesman told him to stop calling and finally admitted that most of the sales agents thought Frederick was mentally unstable because he was married to a black woman.[5]

"They thought he was out of his mind," said Chris, who heard the story many times when he was older. The grievances weren't discussed until years later when wounds had healed and the children were grown.

Frederick and Elinor carried on as if they had never been insulted or rejected. There were never any memorable or animated discussions about race in the Albert household. They didn't focus on it, because their union represented where they stood on the subject. They were committed to facing the world and their children as a solid unit, even when the prejudice was blatant.

They would not let racism impede their ability to provide a good life for their family. If that meant living a life in constant motion in an attempt to keep racism at bay, then that's what Elinor and Frederick did. When Morton no longer worked for them, they left, just as they had done with Göttingen, and Boston before that.

They were running away from racism, an impossible feat. Jim Crow and other discriminatory barriers were there to greet them every time they moved. During the 1950s, interracial marriages were still quite threatening to many. They represented an undoing of what was considered normal, which was "sticking with your own kind."[6] Society left no ambiguity on the issue. As of 1951, twenty-nine states legally barred interracial marriages between blacks and whites. Most were in the South, but that didn't mean northern states didn't subscribe to the same racist views. It just indicated that the black population in those locations was small or interracial marriage was so rare that no legal statutes were put in place. Judges could still deny a marriage license to a mixed-race couple for a host of reasons.[7]

Elinor and Frederick moved just a few miles away to the suburb of Media, where they rented a small two-story house that Elinor decorated with midcentury modern furnishings. And Frederick decided to make a career change. He wasn't going to be a mechanic all his life. Artistry of any kind was his passion, and Frederick believed there was an opportunity in the culinary arts. His knack for baking had gotten him through two years of imprisonment during the war, and in 1954 he decided to return to the kitchen. He applied for a scholarship to the American Institute of Baking in Chicago, and he received it. The program required Frederick to move there for one year, leaving Elinor and the children in Pennsylvania.

During this time, Elinor wanted to seek employment as a nurse, particularly while Frederick was away and sending money home from whatever odd job he worked as a baking student. As always, the idea of Elinor being away from the children created stress in the marriage, even though the additional income was helpful. More than the money,

Elinor missed adult contact, having friends, and caring for those in need. She loved being a mother, but she was unfulfilled in other ways. She was eerily in the same position as her mother years before when she was told she could no longer be a schoolteacher as a married woman in Milton, and Elinor began to experience the same angst. However, it had been the law that forced Gladys to stay home, not her husband.

When Christopher was old enough to be in school, Elinor began accepting private nursing jobs, but inevitably she would have to quit each one soon after because of Frederick's reactions. Even though she chose shifts that were the least disruptive to her children's schedules, Frederick acted as if his whole world were unraveling. Elinor finally gave up the idea of working while the children were young. She feared that if the time came when she had to work to support the family, her pattern of accepting employment and quitting would prevent her from being hired.[8]

Elinor also knew that her desire to work made Frederick feel like a failure, incapable of supporting his family, and that weighed on her. During the time they lived in Göttingen she had witnessed firsthand Frederick's lifelong struggle with the rejection he felt from his father. Frederick was the center of her life, and she wanted to keep him happy. She knew she could make him happier by not working, so once again she decided to drop the idea of employment, this time for good.

Frederick excelled at school because he hoped a career in

baking was his ticket to financial stability, but he neglected his family in the process by temporarily living out of state. The same intensity that his own father had for his engineering business, which kept him away from his family, influenced Frederick more than he would have liked to believe. And as with Karl Albert, there were other women in Frederick's life. Chris, too young during this period to know, learned years later that this had been a difficult time in his parents' marriage, either because of other women, long absences, or both.[9]

Elinor and Frederick's marital problems manifested themselves mostly in silence, as evidenced by the fact that no one knew about any strife between them until years after the difficult moments had long passed. They dealt with weaknesses in their relationship similarly to the ways in which they responded to the pain of racism—with stoic calm.

There was no doubt that these two people still desperately loved each other, but figuring out how to establish themselves was difficult, particularly for Elinor. In so many of their living situations, she was isolated and the one who stayed at home by herself with the children.

Although periods of infidelity were woven throughout their marriage, it wasn't clear if Elinor had proof Frederick was cheating on her. She never discussed it with anyone, not even when Chris and Stephen were adults, and she never disparaged Frederick. And although an adulterer, Frederick wasn't cruel the way his father had been—he would never have thrown his infidelity in Elinor's face. Unlike his own father in his relationship with Frederick's mother, Frederick genuinely desired Elinor. But he undoubtedly led a duplicitous life.

After graduation from baking school in 1955, Frederick returned to Pennsylvania—but the family would move again when Frederick received a job offer as an experimental baker at Pepperidge Farm in Connecticut. They settled into a ranch-style home tucked away in a wooded neighborhood in Fairfield County. It was a secluded location, a place of refuge for Frederick, but a questionable choice for anyone with two young boys longing for friends and normalcy and with a sociable wife who missed having girlfriends around.

"My father rented a house. I think the address was Easton Road, and once you come four or five miles inland it becomes very rural," said Chris. Their home backed up to a nearby stream. Though picturesque, it was certainly not a good choice for Stephen, who at age ten had already lived in Massachusetts, Germany, and more than one location in Pennsylvania. There were no playgrounds or baseball fields nearby where the boys could meet kids their age, and the seven-year age gap between Stephen and Chris made it difficult for them to play with each other for very long. This made for especially tedious summers.

Surprisingly, Elinor and Frederick did not spend much time or energy worrying about how Stephen and Chris acclimated to all the different homes, schools, and neighborhoods. In their minds, each time they moved they were getting closer to the track to prosperity. Frederick had found a nice house for his family, and he loved his job at Pepperidge Farm. His career began to soar and he started to make good money. It was only a matter of time before he would have everything he wanted, which he thought would be everything his family wanted. The process of getting there, however, was plagued with long hours and emotional distance from his growing sons, who needed more of their father in their lives. Frederick, though, was focused on his family's financial security. He was relentless in his pursuit of success, as if he was still trying to prove his father wrong.

As the children got older, Elinor and Frederick continued to avoid talking about race. People still stared at them when they got out of their car together or took a booth at a restaurant. There were looks of surprise and whispers, but they never lost their patience or their tempers with gawkers. Elinor and Frederick just focused on themselves. Their marriage was back on track, and for the first time they could feel things working out. The family enjoyed Sunday drives together in the countryside of Connecticut. And Frederick and Elinor showed their love for each other openly.

Two countries, four cities, and at least six different residences. That's how many times Frederick and Elinor packed up and started over after their marriage in 1947. For years they shuffled between rented houses and apartments, trying to find a place that would accept them. Finally in 1959 everything fell into place.

Village Creek, an idyllic waterfront community in South Norwalk, Connecticut, backs up to Long Island

Sound. In 1949, a handful of New Yorkers who wanted a chance to raise their families in an affordable, tranquil, and prejudice-free zone launched a search for the perfect settlement. The group, many of whom were former veterans and avid sailors, also included artists, lawyers, doctors, businessmen, and teachers searching for the American dream they had fought for and could afford. They discovered an uninhabited stretch of land for sale, a peninsula, owned by the Nash Engineering Company. With each family contributing, they secured the property, which spanned seventy-three acres, for a reported $75,000. They divided the land into sixty-nine lots, allotting a third of an acre with scenic views to each house. It was an affordable neighborhood that allowed families to own their own private oasis on the water.[10]

Village Creek quickly developed, and residents enjoyed community tennis courts as well as a shared marina and an idyllic beach on the Long Island Sound.[11] But people who moved there invested in more than scenic homes on the water—they were sending a message. Village Creek was progressive and represented modernity in design and thinking. The homes were mostly midcentury modern, with natural light to take advantage of the beautiful views. And beyond the aesthetics, Village Creek welcomed everyone—something Elinor and Frederick had never experienced as an interracial couple. "Those of us who started Village Creek had a special kind of a community in mind," reads the Village Creek's 1951 prospectus. "We were looking for a good place in which to live and bring up our children, a community which would be in itself a model of democracy. We wanted a healthful place to live, waterfront, view . . . but above all else we wanted a community with a completely democratic character—no discrimination because of race, color, creed or politics." [12]

The neighborhood seemed too good to be true, too utopian and unrealistic, and there was some backlash. Real estate brokers didn't share the village's vision of diversity, and for the first ten years of the neighborhood's existence, agents refused to show any houses to white families once word spread that the community allowed blacks.

One of the Village Creek founders, Roger Wilcox, recalled the pushback he received for showing some of the plots to an African American family. "I couldn't get FHA insurance for mortgages. We were told flatly that we would have to get rid of our covenants if we wanted FHA mortgage insurance," he said. The covenant included a commitment to maintaining a racial balance in Village Creek, and every member had to sign it. "I told them, 'We are a cooperative and we are not going to change our covenants.' The covenants were the whole basis for why we were there in the first place. And they said, 'Then you don't get any loans.'" [13]

Homes in Village Creek were advertised mostly by word of mouth—and it worked. Even though mortgages were hard to obtain because Norwalk banks feared the community would become "too black," the residents thrived, and

Village Creek lived up to its goals. It maintained a healthy balance of white, black, and mixed-race neighbors.[14]

Elinor and Frederick purchased a split-level house in Village Creek, on Split Rock Road, and settled into a community where they finally could walk hand in hand down the street without feeling self-conscious. There were even neighborhood children, white and black, for Chris and Stephen to befriend. For the first time since they married, Elinor and Frederick had found a welcoming neighborhood. Just a year prior to their move, in 1958, a Gallup poll recorded that only 4 percent of white Americans approved of interracial marriages.[15] Elinor and Frederick had found a community that fell into that small percentage.

The children were thrilled. There were trails and playgrounds where kids could hang out for hours. Chris and Stephen rode their bikes up and down the street and visited their friends anytime they wanted. There were always community parties where neighbors came together for picnics and sports.[16]

But the utopian environment couldn't erase prejudice beyond the neighborhood. Chris, because he was much younger, didn't experience as many socially isolating moments as Stephen apparently did. He had been a toddler during the period when the family moved frequently. As both children got older, however, the question of where they fit in was subconsciously planted in their minds. Elinor and Frederick didn't actively acknowledge that their sons were in fact different from their classmates. It was something Chris would discover on his own.

When he was seven or eight years old, Chris was getting dressed in the locker room for gym class. Intense conversations were hardly common in second grade, but his friends Joe Johnson and Robert Little were certainly having one.

"All of a sudden they got into a real animated discussion," said Chris. "And they went back and forth and I was kind of listening. And finally Robert Little said, 'Well, his mother's black so he's got to be black.' " That was the first time Chris noticed he was different. It had never occurred to him to ask his parents about his racial identity, because Frederick and Elinor never discussed it. Being mixed-race had never come up.

The way Elinor and Frederick were raising their sons—with no open dialogue about identity—inadvertently created distance between the parents and their children. Something was missing in the Albert household, and the lack of acknowledgment of racism and their unique family characteristics contributed to that. There was a division in the home. Elinor and Frederick were on one side, totally in love with each other, and the children were on another, emotionally neglected and figuring out how to be half white and half black by themselves.

Elinor and Frederick chose to keep much of their personal story a secret even from their kids. They didn't talk about their time in the army and how they had to sneak around to be together. The two didn't share vivid details about their respective upbringings, family dysfunction, or the social climate of the time. They had programmed the family to function in such a way that it wasn't normal to reveal past grievances, despite the fact that it would have made the children feel much closer to their parents. Conversations that would have seemed obvious to have with the children never happened. With the exception of a few anecdotes, Elinor rarely elaborated on her moments of despair while serving in the U.S. Army Nurse Corps, or her anger toward the military and the people of Arizona, who humiliated her with segregation and discrimination.

Her niece Hope was an adult when she learned about Elinor's time in Göttingen. And that was only because Hope described herself as naturally inquisitive and unafraid to ask her aunt questions, especially about her past, something Chris and Stephen didn't do.

It was clear that Elinor wanted to protect her sons from the evils of racism, and avoiding the topic was one way to do that. She may have feared that if she shared painful moments, her children would begin to expect the worst from people or start to believe that they were different or inferior. But the reality was that outside of Village Creek, the Albert family *was* different. There wasn't a population of black women in the United States who had married German POWs. It was a complete anomaly. And by ignoring the most obvious elements of themselves, Elinor and Frederick didn't prepare Chris and Stephen for the kinds of questions they would encounter at school and in the real world.

Situations that were awkward for Chris as a child were much easier to understand as an adult. Growing up, he thought it was strange that Frederick would always walk ahead of his mother when they entered a restaurant. Being a kid, he figured his father was just in a hurry and walked faster than anyone else in the family. Later, he wondered if his father was distancing himself from Elinor and their two sons to ensure that they would get a table without any problem. "When we'd go out to eat, up until I was at least nine, I wasn't really aware of the dynamic. Here's an interracial family going to sit down at a restaurant in a setting, in most cases in Fairfield County, at least in those days, in which at least 90 percent of the attendants and guests in the restaurant are white." He remembered some stares within the first five minutes of seating—nothing menacing, but "I felt it."[17]

What Elinor and Frederick could do was share their hobbies. For Elinor that was antiquing, mentoring, and gardening; for Frederick, that meant playing jazz, sailing, or painting.

"The closest I ever felt to my father was the period where his hobby was boats, each increasing in size," said Chris. "The first boat he had was a sixteen-foot, then he had a twenty-one-foot, then he had a twenty-three-foot, then he had about a twenty-eight-foot, then he went back to a smaller boat. But there was a period of about a summer or two summers where we would regularly go out, just the two of us. And occasionally my mother would join us."[18] But those moments still never included too much conversation. Usually Frederick sailed alone or went on the boat with just Elinor.

The few times when Frederick was social, he hid it from his children, as if he believed showing a playful side was inappropriate for a parent. Once Chris rode with Elinor to pick up Frederick from work and was shocked to see him holding court with a group of coworkers, everyone laughing. "I never really saw that social side of him."

"You'd assume a father and son—every weekend—would have some kind of project. Fixing the car, working on the house," Chris went on. But what would begin as an endearing father-son moment with Frederick would usually end with one of his sons getting his feelings hurt. Chris remembered that when Frederick was working on one of his cars, occasionally he would need a tool to help him repair something in the engine. "I'd say, 'Hey, Pops, you want some help?' He'd say, 'Hand me that number two wrench,' and 'Hand me this.' Then it'd be about three to five minutes before I'd hand him the wrong tool and he'd say 'Hell, get away from here!' "[19]

Frederick wasn't intentionally cold like his father, but he struggled with showing affection to his children, and he displayed a level of intolerance that could be cruel and dismissive. He was at home much more often than his father, which could have been why he didn't see himself as hard on his sons. And there was some warmth; the boys received hugs, and for a time Frederick kissed them good night. But Chris remembered that his father abruptly stopped being affectionate when he was around seven or eight years old, and a year went by without Frederick kissing him good night. It must have bothered Elinor, because she told Chris one evening before bed, "Give your father a kiss," and he did. Looking back on it, Chris felt as if she knew that Frederick had created unnecessary boundaries and she didn't want that to continue.

Chris learned to accept his father's reticence. He understood that Frederick's upbringing was largely shaped by Karl's coldness and lack of interest in his own family. "There were no warm experiences," said Chris, about Frederick's relationship with Karl. "The first time my father taught me how to dive or the first time my father taught me how to swim, or the first time I sat on my father's lap when he was driving—none of that stuff was going on."

Frankly, Frederick showed as much affection as he was able to. In comparison to the relationship he had with his own dad, that was an improvement, but it was still not adequate.

"I really noticed as an adult, when I had access to other families and [could] see their closeness, that there is a difference," said Chris.[20]

The fact that Frederick was so much more willing to shower attention on his wife than his children became so obvious that relatives wondered if Elinor and Frederick ever should have had children. They were so into each other that their children seemed secondary. It impacted Stephen the most, who as an adult struggled with periods of estrangement from both of his parents and had no interest in sharing any memories of them.

"It would have been hard for anybody to be Ellie and Frika's child," said Hope. "Frika loved the boys, you know; they were his pride and joy as well. But in terms of affection and open affection, Ellie was the only one. That's a tough thing for a kid to grow up with."[21]

What was clear to everyone around him was that Frederick made Elinor his center of social contact. He didn't have friends or hang out with his colleagues after work. He never came home from the office to drop off his briefcase and say he was running out to have a beer with the guys. He didn't have any "guys." If the phone rang, it was for Elinor, or one of the boys once they were older.

"He never really got a personal, friendly phone call where somebody would call up and they would have a conversation," said Chris, who couldn't recall his father inviting anyone over for a drink, to watch a game, or to listen to music and talk. Elinor was the opposite. She would sit in a chair in the kitchen where there was a wall phone and talk to someone for forty-five minutes. On the rare occasion Frederick had a call, it lasted five minutes at best.

During the holidays when the family drove to New Jersey or the Bronx to visit Elinor's relatives, Frederick was ready to go as soon as the presents were opened or the meal was done. He didn't have any time for just talking and laughing—that didn't come naturally to him. The idea of spending all of Christmas Day at someone else's home was too much for him. No matter how tired the kids were, they always drove home the same day and never spent the night. Frederick was always ready to leave.

It wasn't just family gatherings that made him uncomfortable. Even a neighbor's adult party made Frederick socially awkward. He would talk only to Elinor, which isolated her from other people, the last thing she wanted.

"My mom, she liked to dance," said Chris. "In fact, that was always a point of—it wasn't a disagreement, it's just that my father was self-conscious of the fact that, you know, he's German, and he didn't have a sense of rhythm. A song would come on and he'd be clapping to the wrong beat."

There was something Frederick managed to truly bond with his sons over, and that was his obsession with jazz. He never lost his love for it, and he willingly, openly, and unapologetically shared it with his sons. The good times together as a family revolved around jazz, especially when Stephen and Chris were of the age when they could appreciate the sound. If there ever was a moment when Frederick became animated, it was when jazz was the topic of conversation. When the boys were old enough to play instruments, they challenged their dad on different styles. Chris was more inspired by bebop and post-bop jazz, like Charlie Parker, Dizzy Gillespie, and Miles Davis; Stephen loved Chet Baker. Frederick, however, was exclusively drawn to jazz from New Orleans. The debates were lively and fun.

The three would even have impromptu jam sessions from time to time.[22]

"When he would come home from work, he would have rented either a brass instrument like a trombone or more frequently, a trumpet or clarinet, and then probably before dinner, he would pick up the horn and just play it furiously, in the most musical way he could conjure up," said Chris. "He would put on a record of Louis Armstrong or Sidney Bechet and he would try to play along. But of course with no training or no intuition in terms of any brass technique, one out of every four notes might be right."

There was jazz playing at the Albert house nonstop. Elinor and Frederick played records every single day, all day. The music added warmth to the home, making the lack of communication between the parents and their kids less obvious. Seeing Frederick talkative lifted everyone's spirits, especially Elinor, who was naturally loquacious. She had become a delight to her neighbors and a beloved resident of Village Creek.

Pamela Ballard was a teenager and friends with Stephen when she first met Elinor. "There was a couch, and I would come and sit on that couch in the early afternoon, late morning. I'd be here until about ten of five, until she'd say, 'Oh! I didn't realize—where did the time go? I've got to fix dinner for Frika.' And she'd go running into the kitchen and say, 'You've got to go!' That happened so many days."[23]

Elinor loved taking care of her family and was a gourmet cook. "She could make wiener schnitzel like killer," said

Chris. She sent him to school with decadent sandwiches. While other kids were eating peanut butter and jelly, Chris had roast pork or tuna on homemade bread. She made sure dinner was lavish. She could make every kind of cuisine imaginable, including Bavarian food, which she would fuse with soul food.

Her energy even inspired Frederick to occasionally bake at home. He and Chris would make kaiser rolls and donuts, and eat them fresh out of the oven—one of the few tender moments between them.

Since Elinor had long given up the idea of working, she put her energy into gardening. For years she wore her white nurse's jacket and would sit on a stool weeding and planting for hours and "sweating like a pig," said Chris. She tended to the garden almost every day; that became her job. When Frederick left for work, Elinor went to her yard. Tomatoes, corn, flowers, exotic plants, perennials—she cultivated a beautiful garden that neighbors stopped by to admire.

Elinor was always caring for something or someone. She was a nurturer, and her garden reflected that. She never burdened anyone with her problems, but she was always around to listen to theirs. Teenage girls frequently visited her, and she showered them with gifts—dresses or jewelry. She was an avid collector of art and antiques, as well as a mentor and volunteer at Planned Parenthood. As long as Elinor was taking care of someone, obviously Frederick first, she was happy.

As the children grew older and the civil rights movement

became more pronounced, the Albert family still functioned in their bubble of racial avoidance. Elinor didn't participate in protests and didn't have any talks with her sons about what it meant to be black in America. There were no references to the March on Washington, Martin Luther King Jr., or Malcolm X. She once made a comment that they would never travel to the South, which irked some of her family who lived in Virginia. There were never any family outings to protests, or any acknowledgment that mixed marriages still weren't legal in several states and would remain so until 1967.[24]

And Frederick continued his infidelity.

Chris remembered that when he was a young teenager he once saw his father riding as a passenger in a woman's car at a time when Frederick should have been at work. Once he saw Frederick duck, he realized that his father and the woman were engaged in something illicit. When Chris returned home and saw his father later that night, the two exchanged a lingering look that was an acknowledgment of what had happened, as well as an unspoken act of solidarity ensuring that Chris would not mention it to Elinor. And he never did.[25]

Flawed marriage and all, Elinor and Frederick remained devoted to each other. She knew that Frederick would never leave her for another woman, because she was the most important person in his life. They had been through too much together and were completely dependent on each other.

Even if Elinor wanted to leave Frederick because of his cheating, it would have been very difficult. He provided everything, so much so that Elinor didn't even know how to write a check.[26] "You know the sun rose and set in Ellie," said Hope about Frederick's feelings toward her aunt. "I mean, they did their bickering-back-and-forth kind of thing, but there was nothing that she could want and that she didn't have."[27] The fire was still present in their marriage, she was in love with him despite his many flaws, and she was accustomed to her comfortable life.

Chris had started taking private trumpet lessons at age twelve or thirteen. Although Frederick was skeptical of his son's talent, Elinor was an immediate fan, and Chris's instructors lauded him for his perfect pitch. But Frederick's doubts left an impression on his son. "In the first three or four years of playing, he said, 'Well, if you can't play what you hear, then you might as well quit now.' And that came on very strong, because when someone says something to you with that much absolute attitude, it's like, 'Well, maybe I should give up.' "[28] He didn't quit, but a rift grew between the two men.

As a teenager in the 1960s, Chris found it harder to exist in the color-blind world that Elinor and Frederick created. He read the *Autobiography of Malcolm X* and became intrigued by the Black Power Movement. At fourteen, Chris began to embrace his black heritage more openly than his white side. He wore an Afro and went to school wearing dashikis.

"I became kind of self-conscious about being in public with my father and having one of my black friends say, 'Oh your father is white.' Like it wouldn't be obvious anyway that one of my parents was white. But I went through this period, at least three or four years, like I was kind of on alert when we'd ride around in the car." Frederick didn't say anything about his son's increasingly moody attitude, but it became so troubling to Elinor that she confronted Chris. She looked her son straight in the eye and told him, "Don't make me choose between the two of you. Because I'm going to choose him."

That moment stuck with Chris. He interpreted Elinor as telling him to respect his father—and that she was more concerned with how Frederick felt than about appreciating the difficult position her son was navigating as a mixed-race child during intense social unrest. "Ten years later I could say, 'Well, yes, it's important that if you have elements of your DNA and personality that you have to acknowledge whatever you're made up of,' " said Chris. However, it was clear to the teenage Chris that his mother didn't understand.[29]

Frederick may have avoided the issue of race because, as a white man, he simply had no idea how to comfort his son. He may have felt guilt for not being able to understand what being half black meant in a racist society. Or he didn't want to unleash emotions and problems for which he didn't have a solution.

Chris was accepted into and attended the New England

Conservatory of Music. Elinor and Frederick drove up for his final graduation concert. Chris knew his father was still ambivalent about his talent, but Frederick dutifully attended and took a seat in the auditorium alongside the other parents. Before Chris went onstage Elinor said to him, "Play pretty for the people." And he did just that, churning out a melodious rendition of "Stella by Starlight." "I remember my mother was proud and said, 'That was beautiful, Christopher.'" He didn't expect a compliment from Frederick, nor did he remember getting one. But by then, Chris had accepted his father on Frederick's terms. He knew his dad wasn't going to gush over him, ever—he didn't know how.

Chris continued to pursue his music and didn't look back, traveling the world playing the trumpet. On the rare occasion he stopped home in between gigs and practiced in his old room, Elinor stood by the door, listening to him play and getting choked up.

Once the children moved out, Elinor and Frederick kept up their routine. Frederick had become a vice president at Pepperidge Farm, where during his time overseeing the experimental bakery, the famous Pepperidge Farm apple pie tart was created.[30] However, the company couldn't confirm if Frederick personally developed the recipe, which was similar to the dessert he used to make for Elinor when he was a POW.

Frederick had long since patched up his relationship with his mother, traveling to Europe over the years to visit. After Karl Albert died in 1964, Margarete took several trips of her own, including one to Village Creek, and developed a far more congenial disposition in her later years. She and Elinor were cordial to each other, although never close, and that was the extent of their relationship until Margarete's death in 1991.[31]

Elinor continued to garden, have friends over in the afternoon, cook dinner for Frederick, and listen to Louis Armstrong, Sidney Bechet, and Duke Ellington in the evenings in the living room with Frederick. That part of their lives would never change. There was always great music playing in the Albert house—the two of them with jazz in the backdrop, just as it had been from the start.

"They loved each other deeply until the day they died," said Chris.

Postscript

IN 1981, CHRIS ALBERT JOINED THE COUNT BASIE Band, and by 1999, he was a trumpet player in the Duke Ellington Orchestra, though neither Frederick nor Elinor would ever see him perform on that level. Frederick, like his father, was diagnosed with Parkinson's disease and died in June 2001, at age seventy-five. Elinor, who had been in poor health for a while, died four years later from a cancerous growth in her chest, at age eighty-four.

Chris came to accept that there were parts of Frederick and Elinor's lives that he would never fully know.

"I think there's a certain amount of programming that goes on in family and long-term relationships," he said. "You know what to expect and for instance, now that I'm a middle-aged person, and even years before, I said, 'Well, why didn't I ever ask him about Hitler? And why didn't I ever ask him about the whole Nazi movement?'"[1]

Stephen Albert, in a rare moment of talking about his parents, agreed. "When I think back on it, they didn't volunteer a lot, let's put it that way. And I don't think I particularly asked a lot either. It's not like they were hiding anything, but they just didn't bring it up."[2]

Stephen, who chose not to participate in the research for this book, went on to have a career in social work, before retiring in South Norwalk, Connecticut, where he lives. Chris resides in the family house in Village Creek. He toured with the Duke Ellington Orchestra until 2017.

"My father didn't talk much. And my mom didn't reveal that much either. But at least my parents gave me jazz."

Acknowledgments

THIS BOOK EXISTS, QUITE SIMPLY, BECAUSE THERE are people in my life who believe in me and never hesitate to help me. From family and friends to professional colleagues, as well as a ton of prayer, I cannot stress how grateful I am for the support system that helped *Enemies in Love* come to be.

My mind doesn't think chronologically when it comes to all the people I want to thank and all the enriching experiences I've had while writing this book. But I'm forever grateful to Chris Albert, Elinor and Frederick's youngest son, who couldn't have been more generous with his time and candid about his parents. I usually took the train up to South Norwalk, Connecticut, in the morning to visit Chris at his house in Village Creek, listening to jazz in the background and thumbing through Elinor's scrapbooks, while he smoked cigarettes and talked about his parents. This book couldn't have happened without him.

Another person who helped make this project happen is my wonderful agent Howard Yoon, of the Ross Yoon Agency, who loved this story just as much as I did and helped me envision the very book I wanted to write.

I'm also forever indebted to Darren Walker, president of the Ford Foundation. His support of my book through grants allowed me to travel to Europe numerous times, as well as to several places within the United States to conduct interviews and research.

To the editors of this book, Cecelia Cancellaro and New Press executive editor Marc Favreau, I am so grateful to you both for your comments, questions, strikethroughs, deletions, you name it. Your feedback and attention to detail were invaluable. And thank you to everyone else at The New Press for believing in this book—in particular, publisher Ellen Adler, editorial director Carl Bromley and senior managing editor Maury Botton.

From a personal standpoint, I'm so appreciative of my family and friends who kept me going in more ways than one. Thank you to my wonderful parents, Ben and Jennifer Clark, who've encouraged me to write from the moment I picked up a pen. It's an incredible feeling to have parents who think you're amazing and highly capable and I thank God for them every day. I also want to thank for their continuous support: my brothers Ben and Steven Clark, sister-in-law Sharon Clark, my aunt Olivia Robinson, and my fairy godmothers Renée Paige and Sande Robinson.

There are a handful of friends who have heard me talk about this book for the last five years. And those same friends have also talked me off a ledge because of this book. Their friendship and encouragement were vital when I hit a dead end, had writer's block, or just freaked out about anything I could think of at the time: Shellie Anders, Marshall Mitchell, Susan Fales-Hill, Shoshana Guy, Anne Simmons, Yolanda Griffin, Keli Goff, Subrata De, Gillian Miniter, and DeMarco Morgan.

I want to thank all the family and friends of Elinor and Frederick whom I met or spoke to, no matter how briefly, on this journey: Charlotte Tutsek, Hope Taylor, Alethea Felton, Anne Felton, Dina Felton, Stephen Albert, Chan Albert, Jill Williams, Edward Allen, Pamela Ballard, Piroschka Dossi, and Diana Dickson.

In particular, I want to thank Kristina Brandner, the daughter of Charlotte Tutsek, Frederick's sister. As with Chris, I developed a friendship with Kristina, who was so generous with her time and very honest about her family's dynamics. Whether we were on one of our long walks through Munich's Olympic Park, sitting on her botanical-adorned terrace, or at a beer garden, she shared her family's history and I am so grateful to her for that. Kristina also served as translator when I met with Charlotte. In her mid-nineties, always impeccably dressed, Charlotte welcomed me into her lovely Munich apartment a few times, where we sat in her living room and talked over coffee and sweets served on fine china.

With the timing of this book, sadly, most of the black nurses who served in World War II have passed on. But I managed to meet Elinor's friend from Camp Florence, Gwyneth Blessitt Moore, and can't thank her enough for talking to me. She had read my story about Elinor and Frederick in the *New York Times* and reached out to Chris, who in turn passed on my contact information. She was the only person I had found who witnessed Elinor and Frederick falling in love.

I also had several phone calls with former army nurse Dorothy Jenkins, who served at Camp Papago Park in Arizona during the war. She provided some powerful anecdotes about her time there, and I'm thankful for her openness to share with me.

A tremendous amount of research was required for this book. There are several institutions that I want to acknowledge: the National Archives at College Park in Maryland; the Library of Congress; the New York Public Library; the Schomburg Center for Research in Black Culture; the German Historical Institute in Washington, D.C., and in London; Amistad Research Center at Tulane University; Moorland-Spingarn Research Center at Howard University; Western Reserve Historical Society in Cleveland; Fondren Library at Southern Methodist University; and the World War II Museum in New Orleans.

Also, a special thank-you to Dan Haacker of the Milton Historical Society for helping me track down all things related to the Powells—birth records, marriage certificates, obituaries, real estate records, and newspaper clippings. Confirming many of the Powell family's biographical details couldn't have been done without his help.

This book also took me to Fort Huachuca, in Arizona. It was my first time on a military base and I had no idea where to go and how to search for archives. Thank you to Ret. General Julius Parker for answering my email and putting me in touch with Charles Hancock and Harlan Bradford, two veterans and members of the Southwest Association of Buffalo Soldiers who were stationed at Fort Huachuca decades ago, and who took me on a tour of the installation. Thank you also to Dr. Kate Schmidli of the Fort Huachuca Museum.

Another base I visited was Fort Sam Houston in San Antonio, which houses an impressive number of records of military nurses. Thank you to Col. Elizabeth Vane and archivist Carlos Alvarez for helping me sort through the material at the AMEDD Center of History and Heritage at Fort Sam Houston.

I relied on a number of books and papers written by various academics and historians. In some cases, I was able to interview the authors or exchange emails. I'd like to thank the following people in those categories: Professor Matthias Reiss of the University of Exeter; Steve Hoza, a military historian based in Arizona; Professor Charissa Threat of Spelman College; Professor Emeritus Arnold Krammer of Texas A&M; Professor Richard F. Wetzell, research fellow at the German Historical Institute in Washington, D.C.;

Professor Heide Fehrenbach of Northern Illinois University; Professor Marvin Dulaney of the University of Texas at Arlington; Barbara Schmitter Heisler, professor emerita of Gettysburg College; Professor David Imhoof of Susquehanna University; and Barbara Brooks Tomblin, author of *G.I. Nightingales: The Army Nurse Corps in World War II.* And thank you to Sarah Huebinger, who translated and transcribed many of my interviews.

Thank you to Diego Ribadeneira and the *New York Times* for publishing my article about Elinor and Frederick back in 2013. I'm convinced that having a byline in the *Times* is what a journalist dreams of.

I also want to thank Columbia University Graduate School of Journalism. As an alum, as well as a current adjunct, I know I'm a better reporter and writer for having walked through those prestigious doors as a student many years ago. Before Columbia, I went to the University of Virginia for a graduate program in government. It was rigorous and challenging and helped prepare me for the research process for this book.

I also had the great fortune to attend wonderful schools growing up in Dallas, Texas. Thank you to the Lamplighter School and the Greenhill School—two very special places that made getting an education an extraordinary experience. I truly cherish those years.

I'd like to acknowledge *Town & Country* magazine, in particular former editor in chief Pamela Fiori, the late editor at large Michael Cannon, and former special correspondent

William Norwich—the most wonderful bosses I could ever have. Several years ago when I worked there, as an editor covering social and philanthropic events, I was out on the town representing the magazine several nights a week. I had to talk to different people all the time at events that I usually attended alone—cocktail parties, black-tie galas. It didn't matter how anxious I felt that night, it didn't matter how unfriendly or obnoxious my dinner companions were—and thankfully that rarely happened—I had to talk and observe, because that was my job. That experience helped me manage any trepidation I had interviewing people for this book.

And I don't know if I could have done that job as effectively if it hadn't been for the four glorious years I spent at my alma mater, Spelman College, where women are taught to be fearless. I received a stellar education there and made wonderful friends, including my sorority sisters of Delta Sigma Theta, Eta Kappa chapter, who are my cheerleaders, therapists, and advisers whenever I need them.

As mentioned above, *Enemies in Love* required years of research. Given the subject matter, I experienced a range of emotions while writing this book. I started watching documentaries on Hitler; I felt it would help me better understand the world in which Frederick grew up. Night after night, I stared at my television in horror, looking at archival videos of a monster. My stomach knotted up at footage of the Holocaust and I remember my own sadness walking around the grounds of Dachau Concentration Camp during one of my trips to Munich.

I also felt a heaviness reading the oral histories of black nurses and soldiers who honorably served this country during the war while facing habitual humiliation. I am forever grateful for their patriotism and courage.

When I think about Elinor and Frederick falling in love against a backdrop of racism, I admire them even more. I thank them for following their hearts. It was an honor to write their story.

Notes

1. Elinor

1. "Harlem 1900–1940," New York Public Library, Schomburg Center for Research in Black Culture, digital exhibition, 2002, exhibitions .nypl.org/harlem.

2. U.S. Census Data, Milton, Massachusetts, 1940.

3. Ella Wade and William Powell marriage license, Massachusetts, Town and Vital Records, ancestrylibrary.com; Alethea Felton interview, April 7, 2013.

4. Alethea Felton interview, April 7, 2013.

5. Milton Historical Society, Massachusetts Historical Commission, drawing and history of 114 Granite Place.

6. *Milton Record*, May 24, 1924, 3.

7. Albert Kendall Teele, *The History of Milton, Mass., 1640 to 1887* (Boston: Rockwell and Churchill, 1887), 31–40; "Town of Milton," www .townofmilton.org/about/pages/history.

8. "Walter Baker & Co. General History," *Dorchester Atheneum*, May 17, 2005, www.dorchesteratheneum.org/page.php?id=553.

9. Suffolk Resolves, 1774.

10. U.S. Census Data, Boston, 1880.

11. "Population Trends in Boston: 1640–1990," *Boston History and Architecture*, www.iboston.org/mcp.php?pid=popFig.; Mark R. Schneider, *Boston Confronts Jim Crow 1890–1920* (Boston: Northeastern University Press, 1997), 4.

12. Isabel Wilkerson, *The Warmth of Other Suns* (New York: Vintage Books, 2010).

13. James Oliver Horton and Lois Horton, *Black Bostonians: Family Life and Community Struggle in the Antebellum North* (New York: Holmes & Meier, 1999), 73–74.

14. Horton and Horton, *Black Bostonians*, 158–159; Mark R. Schneider, *Boston Confronts Jim Crow, 1890–1920.*

15. Hope Taylor interview, October 24, 2014.

16. *Milton Record* obituary for John D. Powell, December 10, 1910. Obit includes mention of John T. Powell of the 39th Regiment, USCT, MD.

17. Entry for Ray Elliott in "American Centuries: Views from New England," Memorial Hall Museum's online collection, www.american centuries.mass.edu/centapp/oh/story.do?shortName=elliot1917.

18. *Milton Record*, October 26, 1918.

19. Equal Justice Initiative, *Lynchings in America: Confronting the Legacy of Racial Terror*, 2nd ed. (Montgomery, AL: Equal Justice Initiative, 2015).

20. Claudia Goldin, "Marriage Bars: Discrimination Against Married Women Workers," Working Paper, National Bureau of Economic Research, October 1988.

21. Hope Taylor interview, October 24, 2014.

22. Elinor's baby book, written entries by Gladys Powell, 1921.

23. "Two Parent Household: Black Family Structure in Late Nineteenth Century Boston," Elizabeth H. Fleck, *Journal of Social History* 6, no. 1 (Autumn 1972): 3–31

24. Elinor's yearbook entry, Milton High School yearbook, 1938.

25. Milton High School yearbook, 1938, 45.

26. Lincoln School for Nurses collection, Schomburg Center for Research in Black Culture, New York Public Library, archives.nypl.org/scm/20728.

27. Chris Albert interview. May 8, 2012; Chris Albert email to Alexis Clark, August 16, 2017.

2. Frederick

1. Oppeln facts. Municipal Visitor Center, Opole, info.um.opole.pl /en/.

2. Article 231, War Guilt Clause, Treaty of Versailles. "The Dawes Plan, the Young Plan, German Reparations, and Inter-Allied War Debts," Office of the Historian, Department of State, United States of America, history.state.gov/milestones/1921-1936/dawes.

3. Richard J. Evans. *The Third Reich in History and Memory* (London: Little Brown, 2015), 18.

4. John Simkin, "Dawes Plan," Spartacus Educational, September 1997, spartacus-educational.com/GERdawes.htm.

5. John Simkin, "Unemployment in Nazi Germany," Spartacus Educational, September 1997, spartacus-educational.com/GERunemploy ment.htm.

6. "Opole, Poland," Jewish Gen, an affiliate of the Museum of Jewish Heritage, data.jewishgen.org/wconnect/wc.dll?jg~jgsys~community ~-519973; "Opole," Virtual Shtetl, December 2015, www.sztetl.org.pl /en/article/opole/5,history.

7. Charlotte Tutsek interview, November 30, 2015.

8. Kristina Brandner interview, November 30, 2015.

9. Charlotte Tutsek interview, July 18, 2015.

10. Charlotte Tutsek interview, November 30, 2015.

11. "The German Reichsarbeitdienst, Feldgrau.com, German Armed Forces Research, 1918–1945, 1996, www.feldgrau.com/WW2-Ger man-National-Work-Service-Reichsarbeitdienst.

12. Chris Albert interview, May 8, 2012.

13. Kristina Brandner interview, June 22, 2012; Kristina Brandner email to Alexis Clark August 16, 2017.

14. Frederic Spotts, *Hitler and the Power of Aesthetics* (Woodstock, NY: Overlook Press, 2003), 163–164.

3. Fighting Hitler and Jim Crow

1. *Huachuca Illustrated: A Magazine of the Fort Huachuca Museum* 9 (1993): 7.

2. Isabel Wilkerson, *The Warmth of Other Suns* (New York: Vintage Books, 2010), 8–9.

3. Andy A. Beveridge, "Harlem's Shifting Population," *Gotham Gazette*, September 2, 2008.

4. "Harlem Riots of 1943," Weissman Center for International Business, Baruch College, www.baruch.cuny.edu/nycdata/disasters/riots -harlem_1943.html.

5. Claudia Marie Calhoon, "Tuberculosis, Race, and the Delivery of Health Care in Harlem, 1922–1939," *Radical History Review* 80 (Spring 2001): 101–119.

6. Robert C. Hayden, "Historical Overview of Poverty Among Blacks in Boston 1950–1990," *Trotter Review* 17, no. 1 (September 21, 2007): 14.

7. U.S. Census Data, New York, 1940, www.census.gov/population /www/documentation/twps0076/NYtab.pdf.

8. U.S. Census Data, Arizona. 1940, www.census.gov/population /www/documentation/twps0076/AZtab.pdf.

9. Letter to Mabel Staupers from a nurse at P/W Camp Papago Park, Phoenix, Arizona, November 19, 1944, Moorland-Spingarn Collection, Howard University; Ralph A. Storm, *Camp Florence Days* (Eau Claire, Wisconsin: ECPrinting, 2006), 14.

10. Legion of Merit, Colonel Edwin N. Hardy, Headquarters, Army Services Forces, Washington D.C., Fort Huachuca Museum archives.

11. *Huachuca Illustrated* 9 (1993): 88–89.

12. Ibid., 7.

13. Ibid., 84.

14. Darlene Clark Hine. *Black Women in White: Racial Conflict and Co-operation in the Nursing Profession 1890–1950* (Bloomington: Indiana University Press, 1989), 6.

15. "History in Brief," Spelman College official website. www.spelman .edu/about-us/history-in-brief; Hine, *Black Women in White*, 8.

16. Hine, *Black Women in White*, 8–10, 54.

17. Ibid., 6.

18. Mabel Keaton Staupers, *No Time for Prejudice: A Story of the Integration of Negroes in Nursing in the United States* (New York: Macmillan, 1961), 97–98.

19. Ibid., 99.

20. Ibid., 99–100.

21. Hine, *Black Women in White*, 117–120.

22. Telegram to President Roosevelt from Mabel K. Staupers. January 6, 1945, NAACP General File, Library of Congress.

23. "James Carre Magee, Major General, U.S. Army, the Surgeon General," *Army Medical Bulletin* 49 (July 1939): 1–3; Roderick M. Engert, "A Concise Biography of Major General James Carre Magee. Medical Corps, U.S. Army," U.S. Army Medical Department, Office of Medical History, June 1964, history.amedd.army.mil/surgeongenerals/J_Magee .html.

24. Staupers, *No Time for Prejudice*, 102–103; Hine, *Black Women in White*,166; *Huachuca Illustrated* 9 (1993): 41.

25. Barbara Brooks Tomblin, *G.I. Nightingales: The Army Nurse Corps in World War II* (Lexington: University Press of Kentucky, 2003), 194.

26. Gordon R. Sullivan, *The Army Nurse Corps* (Washington, D.C.: U.S. Army Center of Military History, 1993), 6; *Huachuca Illustrated: A Magazine of the Fort Huachuca Museum* 9 (1993): 70.

27. Letters to Walter White, NAACP General File, Camp Conditions A642, Box 11, Folder 9, Library of Congress.

28. *Huachuca Illustrated* 9 (1993): 84.

29. Ibid., 20, 41.

30. Ibid., 20.

31. Ibid., 34.

32. Harlan Branford and Charles Hancock interview, June 11, 2012; Matthias Reiss, "Solidarity Among 'Fellow Sufferers': African Americans and German Prisoners of War in the United States During World War II," *Journal of African-American History* 98, no. 4 (Fall 2013): 542–543.

33. *Huachuca Illustrated* 9 (1993): 45.

34. Ibid., 45.

35. Ibid., 65.

36. Charissa J. Threat. *Nursing Civil Rights* (Champaign: University of Illinois Press, 2015), Appendix A: Facts About Negro Nurses and the War.

37. Tomblin, *G.I. Nightingales*, 196.

4. German POWs in the United States

1. "By the Numbers: The U.S. Military," National World War II Museum, New Orleans, www.nationalww2museum.org/learn/education /for-students/ww2-history/ww2-by-the-numbers/us-military.html.

2. "The Pima Cotton Boom," *The Arizona Experience*, arizona experience.org/remember/pima-cotton-boom; "History of Goodyear," *Goodyear,* www.goodyearaz.gov/about-us/demographics-growth /history-of-goodyear

3. Arnold Krammer, *Nazi Prisoners of War in America* (New York: Stein & Day, 1979), 271–272; Arnold Krammer, "Japanese Prisoners of War," *Pacific Historical Review* 52, no. 1 (February 1983): 70.

4. Some scholars, specifically Arnold Krammer, Michael R. Waters, Matthias Reiss, Barbara Schmitter Heister, Lewis H. Carlson, and Steve Hoza, have written in-depth about German POWs in the United States.

5. Krammer, *Nazi Prisoners of War in America*, 1–2.

6. Ralph A. Storm, *Camp Florence Days* (Eau Claire, Wisconsin: EC Printing, 2006), 25.

7. Krammer, *Nazi Prisoners of War in America*, 2.

8. Matthias Reiss, "Solidarity Among 'Fellow Sufferers': African Americans and German Prisoners of War in the United States During World War II," *Journal of African-American History* 98, no. 4 (Fall 2013): 538.

9. There had been German prisoners of war detained in the United States during the Great War, but many of those POWs were German sailors caught by U.S. forces in Guam. The War Department designated three POW camps for them: Forts Oglethorpe and McPherson in Georgia and Fort Douglas in Utah. The exact number of German prisoners of war in the United States from the Great War wasn't accurately cal-culated, because POWs were detained in the same camps as civilians of German descent who were rounded up and interned on U.S. soil during the war, but the numbers hover around 1,346. Allen Kent Pow-ell, *World War I and Utah*, Utah History Encyclopedia, 1994, heritage .utah.gov/tag/fort-douglas; Leisa N. Vaughn, *The Georgia Hun in the Georgia Sun: German Prisoners of War in Georgia*, Georgia Southern Uni-versity, Jack N. Averitt College of Graduate Studies, Electronic Theses and Dissertations, Spring 2016, 33, digitalcommons.georgiasouthern.edu /cgi/viewcontent.cgi?article=2456&context=etd.

10. Reiss, "Solidarity," 533–534.

11. Krammer, *Nazi Prisoners of War in America*, 93–94.

12. Storm, *Camp Florence Days*, 37; Steven Mintz, *Mexican Americans and the Great Depression* (New York: The Gilder Lehrman Institute of Ameri-can History, 2009–2017), www.gilderlehrman.org/history-by-era/gre at-depression/resources/mexican-americans-and-great-depression.

13. Krammer, *Nazi Prisoners of War in America*, 4.

14. POW registration card for Friedrich Karl Albert. July 9, 1944.

15. Krammer, *Nazi Prisoners of War in America*, 2–3.

16. Ibid., 4–5.

17. Ibid., 3.

18. Ibid., 5.

19. Steve Hoza, *PW: First-Person Accounts of German Prisoners of War In Arizona* (Phoenix: E6B Publications, 1995), 18, 31, 36.

20. Ibid., 11, 17, 33, 34, 36.

21. Krammer, *Nazi Prisoners of War in America*, 23.

22. Reiss, "Solidarity," 537.

23. Ibid., 538, 545.

24. Lewis H. Carlson, *We Were Each Other's Prisoners: An Oral History of World War II American and German Prisoners of War* (New York: Basic Books, 1997), 21.

25. Krammer, *Nazi Prisoners of War in America*, 25.

26. Hoza, "German POWs," 29.

27. Krammer, *Nazi Prisoners of War in America*, 25.

28. Storm, *Camp Florence Days*, 21.

29. Early ADC History, Florence, Arizona Department of Corrections, corrections.az.gov/adc-history.

30. Storm, *Camp Florence Days*, 12; John Hernandez, "The Magma Arizona Railroad Company," www.copperarea.com/pages/the-magma -arizona-railroad/.

31. Ibid., 38.

32. Ibid., 25.

33. Michael R. Waters, *Lone Star Stalag: German Prisoners of War at Camp Hearne* (College Station: Texas A&M University Press, 2006), 22.

34. Storm, *Camp Florence Days*, 24.

35. Hoza, *PW*, 115–116.

36. Krammer, *Nazi Prisoners of War in America*, 126, 136.

37. "Field Service Report on Visit to Prisoner of War Camp, Florence, Arizona, 26–28 April 1945 by Captain Alexander Lakes," Office of the Provost Marshal General, Prisoner of War Special Projects Division, May 12, 1945, National Archives and Records Administration.

38. Tomas Jaehn. "Unlikely Harvesters: German Prisoners of War as Agricultural Workers in the Northwest," *Montana: The Magazine of Western History* 50, no. 3 (Autumn, 2000): 46–57, www.jstor.org /stable/4520253?seq=1#page_scan_tab_contents.

39. "Field Service Report on Visit to Prisoner of War Camp, Florence, Arizona, 26–28 April 1945 by Captain Alexander Lakes," Office of the Provost Marshal General, Prisoner of War Special Projects Division, May 12, 1945, National Archives and Records Administration.

40. Office of the Provost Marshal General, Prisoner of War Special Projects Division, Point 6: Religious Services, National Archives and Records Administration.

41. Office of the Provost Marshal General, Prisoner of War Special Projects Division, Point 4: Education Program, National Archives and Records Administration.

42. Hoza, "German POWs," 85.

43. Waters, *Lone Star Stalag*, 24.

44. Lewis H. Carlson, *We Were Each Other's Prisoners: An Oral History of World War II American and German Prisoners of War* (New York: Basic Books, 1997), 22.

45. Reiss, "Solidarity," 539.

46. Storm, *Camp Florence Days*, 63.

47. Ibid., 73–74.

5. Camp Florence

1. Lewis H. Carlson, *We Were Each Other's Prisoners: An Oral History of World War II American and German Prisoners of War* (New York: Basic Books, 1997), 23.

2. Gwyneth Moore interview, June 10, 2013.

3. Barbara Brooks Tomblin, *G.I. Nightingales: The Army Nurse Corps in World War II* (Lexington: University Press of Kentucky, 2003), 196.

4. Barbara Heisler Schmitter, "Returning to America: German Prisoners of War and the American Experience," *German Studies Review* 31, no. 3 (October 2008): 540.

5. Matthias Reiss, "Solidarity Among 'Fellow Sufferers': African Americans and German Prisoners of War in the United States During World War II," *Journal of African-American History* 98, no. 4 (Fall 2013): 550.

6. Ibid., 545.

7. Arnold Krammer, *Nazi Prisoners of War in America* (New York: Stein & Day, 1979), 92–93.

8. Reiss, "Solidarity," 539.

9. Ibid., 540.

10. Ibid., 540.

11. "Attitudes of Whites Toward Sharing Facilities with Negroes," Research Branch, Special Service, Division of Services of Supply, War Department, July 30, 1942, Library of Congress, NAACP General File, Box A650, Folder 1.

12. Ralph A. Storm, *Camp Florence Days* (Eau Claire, Wisconsin: ECPrinting, 2006), 34.

13. "U.S. Army Nurse Ora Hicks Oral History," C-SPAN, August 5, 2005, www.c-span.org/video/?289838-1/us-army-nurse-ora-hicks -oral-history.

14. Dorothy Cook Jenkins interview with Alexis Clark, April 16,

2014 and November 6, 2014; "Dorothy Margaret Cook Jenkins," The Veterans History Project, The Library of Congress, October 26, 2011, memory.loc.gov/diglib/vhp/story/loc.natlib.afc2001001.32011/.

15. Anonymous letter to Mabel Staupers, Camp Papago Park, August 1, 1944, Moorland-Spingarn Collection, Howard University.

16. Oneida Stuart interview, Veterans History Project, September 15, 1992.

17. Matthias Reiss interview, October 8, 2012.

18. Steve Hoza, *PW: First-Person Accounts of German Prisoners of War in Arizona* (Phoenix, AZ: E6B Publications, 1995), 59.

19. Ibid.

20. Julian Hartt, "Desert Town Protests 'Coddling' Nazi Prisoners," *Atlanta Constitution*, March 12, 1945, 3.

21. Ibid.

22. "Report of Inspection by Major D.L. Schwieger and Captain Robert W. Mess (Office of the Provost Marshal General) of Prisoner of War Camp, Florence, and PW Branch Camps Mt. Graham and Safford, Arizona," July 10, 1945, National Archives, College Park, MD.

23. Chris Albert interview, May 8, 2012.

24. Richard S. Sears, *V-Discs: A History and Discography* (Westport, CT: Greenwood Press, 1980).

25. Chris Albert interview. May 8, 2012.

26. Alexis Clark, "A Black Nurse, a German Soldier and an Unlikely World War II Romance," *New York Times*, May 15, 2013, cityroom .blogs.nytimes.com/2013/05/15/a-black-nurse-a-german-soldier -and-an-unlikely-wwii-romance.

27. Tomblin, *G.I. Nightingales*, 196.

28. Chris Albert interview, May 8, 2012.

6. A Forbidden Romance

1. Hope Taylor interview, October 24, 2014.

2. Gwyneth Moore interview, July 12, 2013.

3. "100-Year-Old Recalls Life as WWII Army Nurse," *Wounded Times*,

February 26, 2011. www.combatptsdwoundedtimes.org/2011/02/100 -year-old-recalls-life-as-wwii-army.html

4. Barbara Brooks Tomblin, *G.I. Nightingales: The Army Nurse Corps in World War II* (Kentucky: The University Press of Kentucky, 1996), 195.

5. Gwyneth Moore interview, June 10, 2013.

6. Dina Felton interview, April 7, 2013.

7. Hope Taylor interview, October 24, 2014.

8. Kristina Brandner email to Alexis Clark, November 1, 2014.

9. Hope Taylor interview, October 24, 2014.

7. End of War

1. Chris Albert interview, June 29, 2012.

2. Steve Hoza, *PW: First-Person Accounts of German Prisoners of War in Arizona* (Phoenix: E68 Publications, 1995), 18.

3. Albert Deutsch, "Bias Bars Needed Nurses from Bedsides of Wounded," *PM*, December 26, 1944.

4. "Army Still Is Balky On Using Negro Nurses" NAACP General File, Box A648, Folder 1 Medical Corps, Library of Congress.

5. Charissa J. Threat, " 'The Hands That Might Save Them': Gender, Race and the Politics of Nursing in the United States during the Second World War," *Gender & History* 24, no. 2 (August 2012): 456–474

6. Mabel Keaton Staupers, *No Time for Prejudice: A Story of the Integration of Negroes in Nursing in the United States* (New York: Macmillan, 1961), 120–121.

7. Joseph Connor, "Drafting Women," *World War II Magazine*, August 6, 2016, www.historynet.com/drafting-women.htm.

8. Staupers, *No Time for Prejudice*, 120.

9. Ibid., 116.

10. Letter to Mabel Staupers, February 14, 1945, Moorland-Spingarn Collection, Howard University.

11. Cheryl Mullenbach, *Double Victory: How African American Women Broke Race and Gender Barriers to Help Win World War II* (Chicago: Chicago Review Press, 2013) 130.

12. Barbara Brooks Tomblin, *G.I. Nightingales: The Army Nurse Corps in World War II* (Lexington: University Press of Kentucky, 2003), 124.

13. Hope Taylor interview, October 24, 2014.

8. An Uncertain Future

1. Steve Hoza, *PW: First-Person Accounts of German Prisoners of War in Arizona* (Phoenix, AZ: E6B Publications, 1995), 87.

2. "Field Service Report on Visit to Prisoner of War Camp, Florence, Arizona, 26–28 April 1945 by Captain Alexander Lakes," Office of the Provost Marshal General, Prisoner of War Special Projects Division, May 12, 1945, National Archives and Records Administration.

3. "Prisoner of War Censorship Report, European Theater of Operations P/W Censorship Bureau. Military Intelligence Service, Curtis J. Siats, Major, Infantry, Commanding," February 2, 1945.

4. Arnold Krammer, *Nazi Prisoners of War in America* (New York: Stein & Day, 1979), 217.

5. Elaine Raines, "Florence's Prisoner of War Camp," *Arizona Daily Star*, August 27, 2009.

6. Hoza, *PW*, 147.

7. Arnold Krammer email to Alexis Clark, May 23, 2017.

8. Krammer, *Nazi Prisoners of War in America*, 232.

9. Ibid., 232–233.

10. Ibid., 235.

11. Ibid., 228.; Convention Relative to the Treatment of Prisoners of War, Geneva, 27 July 1929. Part IV: End of Captivity, Section II: Liberation and Repatriation at the End of Hostilities, Art. 75.

12. Arnold Krammer email to Alexis Clark, May 23, 2017.

13. Convention Relative to the Treatment of Prisoners of War, Geneva, 27 July 1929. Article 75. Part IV: End of Captivity, Section II: Liberation and Repatriation at the End of Hostilities, Art. 75.; Krammer, *Nazi Prisoners*, 249

14. Krammer, *Nazi Prisoners of War in America*, 233–247.

15. Ibid., 243–244; "Camp Shanks" New York State Military Museum and Veterans Research Center, NYS Division of Military and Naval Affairs, dmna.ny.gov/forts/fortsQ_S/shanksCamp.htm.

16. Krammer, *Nazi Prisoners of War in America*, 247–250.

17. Hoza, *PW*, 146.

18. Ibid., 147.

19. Kristina Brandner email to Alexis Clark, May 21, 2017.

20. Hope Taylor interview, October 24, 2014.

21. Ibid.

22. Luke Harding, "Germany's Forgotten Victims," *Guardian*, October 22, 2003.

23. Kristina Brandner email to Alexis Clark, May 21, 2017.

24. Charlotte Tutsek interview, December 2015.

25. Barbara Schmitter Heisler, *From German Prisoner of War to American Citizen: A Social History with 35 Interviews* (Jefferson, NC: McFarland, 2013), 8.

26. Ibid., 101.

27. Barbara Schmitter Heisler interview, June 2, 2017.

28. Chris Albert interview, May 8, 2012.; Certificate of Marriage, Friedrich Karl Albert and Elinor Elizabeth Powell, June 26, 1947. City of New York, Office of City Clerk, Municipal Building, Manhattan.

29. Hope Taylor interview, October 24, 2014.

30. Chris Albert interview, May 8, 2012.

9. Searching for Acceptance

1. "This Day in Truman History, July 26, 1948, President Truman Issues Executive Order No. 9981 Desegregating the Military," Truman S. Library and Museum, www.trumanlibrary.org/anniversaries/deseg blurb.htm.

2. Darlene Clark Hine. *Black Women in White: Racial Conflict and Co-operation in the Nursing Profession 1890–1950* (Bloomington: Indiana University Press, 1989), 184–185.

3. Hope Taylor interview, October 24, 2014.

4. Dr. Edward Allen interview, January 13, 2013.

5. "Edward William Brooke III, 1919–2015," United States House of Representatives, history.house.gov/People/Detail?id=9905.

6. Milton Cemetery records, Gladys E. Powell.

7. Gladys E. Powell obituary, *Milton Record*, June 4, 1948.

8. Hope Taylor interview, October 24, 2014.

9. Ibid.

10. Kristina Brandner email to Alexis Clark, May 21, 2017; Refratechnik company website, www.refra.com/en/history.

11. David Imhoof, *Becoming a Nazi Town: Culture and Politics in Göttingen Between the World Wars* (Ann Arbor: University of Michigan Press, 2013), 7.

12. Imhoof, *Becoming a Nazi Town*, 13–20; "Göttingen: A Short History," Max Planck Institute For Biophysical Chemistry, www.mpibpc.mpg.de/137260/goehistory.

13. Hope Taylor interview, October 28, 2014.

14. Clarence Lusane, *Hitler's Black Victims: The Historical Experiences of Afro-Germans, European Blacks, Africans, and African-Americans in the Nazi Era* (New York: Routledge, 2002), 55, 90, 110–112, 140–143.; "Blacks During the Holocaust," United States Holocaust Memorial Museum, www.ushmm.org/wlc/en/article.php?ModuleId=10005479.

15. Yara-Colette Lemke Muniz de Faria, "Transatlantic Adoption: Mabel A. Grammer and the Brown Baby Plan," The Civil Rights Struggle, African-American GIs and Germany, www.aacvr-germany.org/index.php?option=com_content&view=article&id=136&Itemid=11; "Homes Needed for 10,000 Brown Orphans," *Ebony*, October 1948, 19, NAACP General File. Library of Congress; Letters from 1946 to Walter White of the NAACP from Les Amis Des Enfants de France, American Committee to Aid the Italian-Negro GI Babies, and W.E.B. Du Bois. NAACP General File, Box 11, A642 "Brown Babies," Library of Congress.; Claudia Levy. "Mabel Grammer Dies," *Washington Post*, June 26, 2002.

16. Heide Fehrenbach, *Race After Hitler: Black Occupation Children in Postwar Germany and America* (Princeton, NJ: Princeton University Press, 2007), 40.

17. Ibid.

18. Ibid., 42.

19. Ibid., 43.

20. Kristina Brandner interview, June 22, 2012.

21. Kristina Brandner email to Alexis Clark, March 20, 2016.

22. Kristina Brandner interview, June 22, 2012.

23. Charlotte Tutsek interview, May 25, 2014.

24. Kristina Brandner interview, June 22, 2012.

25. Kristina Brandner email to Alexis Clark, February 26, 2016.

26. Hope Taylor interview, October 24, 2014.

10. Finally Home

1. Alethea Felton interview, April 7, 2013.

2. Letter to Morton School Board written by Elinor Albert, from personal family scrapbook.

3. Handwritten letter from Josephine L. Shumate of the NAACP to Elinor Albert, May 24, 1954.

4. Hope Taylor interview, May 12, 2016.

5. Hope Taylor interview, October 24, 2014; Chris Albert interview, May 8, 2012.

6. Maria P.P. Root, *Love's Revolution: Interracial Marriages* (Philadelphia: Temple University Press, 2001), 164–165.

7. James R. Browning, "Anti-Miscegenation Laws in the United States," *Duke Law Journal* 1, no. 1 (1951).

8. Alethea Felton interview, April 7, 2013.

9. Chris Albert interview, June 29, 2012. "There was shit that had gone down," said Chris about Frederick's time in Chicago. "My father—he wasn't obviously a man's man but he would fuck around. I think specifically when he went to the Baking Institute, because when he came back, it was like, he was gone for months at a time, and I don't know if it was over a course of six months or a year that he came back. but there was discord that I later learned about."

10. Alberta Eiseman, "Keeping a Post War Dream Alive," *New York Times*, August 4, 1996; Alan Bisbort, "Village of Light," *Connecticut Magazine*, June 2011.

11. Alan Bisbort, "Village of Light."

12. Eiseman, "Keeping a Post War Dream Alive."

13. Bisbort, "Village of Light."

14. Lisa Prevost, "A Planned Community Stays the Course," *New York Times*, September 24, 2010.

15. Gallup Poll, 1958 ("Question: Do you approve or disapprove of marriage between blacks and whites?"), www.gallup.com/poll/163 697/approve-marriage-blacks-whites.aspx.

16. Chris Albert interview, May 8, 2012.

17. Chris Albert interview, August 17, 2012.

18. Ibid., 2012.

19. Chris Albert interview, June 29, 2012.

20. Chris Albert interview, August 17, 2012.

21. Hope Taylor interview, October 24, 2014.

22. Ibid.; Chris Albert interview, June 29, 2012.

23. Pamela Ballard interview, May 8, 2012.

24. In 1967, the Supreme Court ruled that anti-miscegenation laws banning interracial marriages were unconstitutional in *Loving v. Virginia*.

25. Chris Albert interview, May 8, 2012.

26. Alethea Felton interview, April 7, 2013.

27. Hope Taylor interview, October 24, 2014.

28. Chris Albert interview, June 29, 2012.

29. Chris Albert interview. May 7, 2012 and August 17, 2012.

30. Pepperidge Farm ad for new apple pie tart, *Life*, May 1, 1970. Frederick Albert ran product development at Pepperidge Farm during this time. The Pepperidge Farm archivist couldn't confirm which recipes Frederick specifically created.

31. Charlotte Tutsek interview, November 30, 2015.

Postscript

1. Chris Albert interview, August 17, 2012.

2. Stephen Albert interview, June 29, 2012.

Index

About the Author

Previously an editor at *Town & Country* magazine, **Alexis Clark** is a freelance journalist who has written for the *New York Times*, Yahoo, *The Root*, *Condé Nast Traveler*, and other publications. An alumna of Spelman College, Clark holds master's degrees from the University of Virginia and Columbia Journalism School, where she's currently an adjunct professor. She lives in New York City.

Publishing in the Public Interest

Thank you for reading this book published by The New Press. The New Press is a nonprofit, public interest publisher. New Press books and authors play a crucial role in sparking conversations about the key political and social issues of our day.

We hope you enjoyed this book and that you will stay in touch with The New Press. Here are a few ways to stay up to date with our books, events, and the issues we cover:

- Sign up at www.thenewpress.com/subscribe to receive updates on New Press authors and issues and to be notified about local events
- Like us on Facebook: www.facebook.com/newpressbooks
- Follow us on Twitter: www.twitter.com/thenewpress

Please consider buying New Press books for yourself; for friends and family; and to donate to schools, libraries, community centers, prison libraries, and other organizations involved with the issues our authors write about.

The New Press is a 501(c)(3) nonprofit organization. You can also support our work with a tax-deductible gift by visiting www.thenewpress.com/donate.